# METHODOLOGIES
## OF BLACK
# THEOLOGY

# METHODOLOGIES OF BLACK THEOLOGY

Frederick L. Ware

WIPF & STOCK · Eugene, Oregon

Wipf and Stock Publishers
199 W 8th Ave, Suite 3
Eugene, OR 97401

Methodologies of Black Theology
By Ware, Frederick L.
Copyright©2002 The Pilgrim Press
ISBN 13: 978-1-55635-736-7
ISBN 10: 1-55635-736-2
Publication date 12/4/2007
Previously published by The Pilgrim Press, 2002

Grateful acknowledgment for permission to reprint from the following:

James H. Cone, "God Is Black," in *Lift Every Voice: Constructing Christian Theologies from the Underside,* edited by Susan B. Thistlethwaite and Mary P. Engel (Maryknoll, N.Y.: Orbis Books, 1998), © 1998 by Orbis Books for the individual authors.

Anthony B. Pinn, *Why Lord? Suffering and Evil in Black Theology* (New York: Continuum, 1995.)

# Contents

# Preface

**F**OR THE FIRST TIME in American history, a broad and concerted effort has been made over the past three decades to put into print beliefs and conceptions that have for centuries been transmitted orally among African Americans. The black theological movement in the United States is a significant development; yet after several decades of publication, that so few persons are aware of the multiple ways in which African American theology is done, as well as the various themes of interest to scholars in the field, is unfortunate. This book seeks to address that lack of awareness by providing a classification and criticism of methodological perspectives in the academic study, interpretation, and construction of black theology in the United States from 1969 to 1999.

Owing to the historical contingencies that gave rise to the movement, many people limit contemporary African American theology to the notion of liberation theology. The black theological movement arose in the heat of African Americans' struggle for civil rights and amid their cries for black power in the 1960s. Notwithstanding its genesis, from the early years and onward of the black theological movement, other themes besides liberation have emerged. This book maps three trajectories: the Black Hermeneutical, the Black Philosophical, and the Human Sciences schools. Because Charles B. Copher's study, which I discuss in chapter 2, discloses the quest for a "black hermeneutics" as a definitive quality in the earliest shared methodological perspective among black theologians, I call their perspective the Black Hermeneutical School. The entry of philosophers of religion into and the use of philosophy in the field of academic black theology resulted in the creation of the Black Philosophical School. The Human Sciences School came about as historians of religion, theologians of culture, sociologists of religion, and other scholars committed to the academic study of African American religion as a cultural phenomenon in human life entered the field of academic black theology. My scheme of classification demonstrates that (1) liberation, if it is indeed the essential theme of African American theology, does not mean the same thing to all black theologians; (2) two principal alternatives are available for dealing with the theme of liberation (i.e., the Black Hermeneutical and Black Philosophical schools); and (3) an additional methodological perspective exists for understanding African American theology, one that subsumes liberation under the theme of empowerment (i.e., the Human Sciences School).

Liberation is certainly a matter of ultimate concern for African Americans. But themes like mystery, wonder, awe, and transcendence are also present in African American religion and culture. I believe, as does Howard Thurman, that scholars must be open to addressing not only the problem of oppression but also existential issues stemming from sickness, aggression and war, mortality, death, rationality of belief in God, and the nature of religious experience itself.[1] Black theologians will continue to nuance the theme of liberation in new and interesting ways. However, scholars must deal with the full range of themes, issues, and concepts in African American religion and culture. The first step toward recognizing multiple religious meanings is dispelling the myth of a homogeneous black theology.

The presence of three schools of academic black theology becomes obvious when the literature of academic black theology is read with a predisposition for appreciating the diversity of thought among black theologians. I have read the literature intentionally avoiding "rational commensuration."

Richard Rorty, a leading contemporary American philosopher, coined the phrase "rational commensuration." Rorty is part of a tradition of philosophical criticism that assesses the plausibility of traditional Western assumptions about knowledge.[2] By "rational commensuration," Rorty means the notion that all contributions to a given discourse or area of inquiry can be brought under one set of norms and/or structural framework of interpretation.[3] He argues that rational commensuration leads toward labeling the thought and perspectives of

---

1. Howard Thurman, *With Head and Heart: The Autobiography of Howard Thurman* (New York: Harcourt Brace Jovanovich Publishers, 1979), 60–61, 259–69.

2. For a summary of this tradition in American philosophy and its relevance to systematic theology, see John E. Thiel, *Nonfoundationalism* (Minneapolis: Fortress Press, 1994).

3. Richard Rorty, *Philosophy and the Mirror of Nature* (Princeton, N.J.: Princeton University Press, 1979), 315–16.

persons differing from the dominant or most prevalent approach to a field of inquiry as erroneous, mistaken, or pretentious. Like Rorty, I am reluctant to normalize discourse — that is to say, to restrict a field of inquiry to one methodology, one set of norms, or one framework.

Like Cornel West, a philosopher in the postanalytic/neopragmatist tradition as is Rorty, I use a method of textual criticism, a close reading and scrutinizing of texts, to show the existence of multiple traditions of thought and practice in African American culture. As a significant figure in the black theological movement, Cornel West has ironically not applied his method of textual criticism to academic black theology as he has to other developments in African American culture. I read the literature of black theology with an appreciation for and expectation of finding diversity of thought. Moreover, I read the literature eyeing disagreements as clues to the existence of more than one model, approach, or perspective for doing black theology.

Chapter 1 gives a brief sketch of black theology. Because detailed histories of academic black theology already exist, I do not retell the entire development of academic black theology. The historical interest of chapter 1 is to define black theology in such a way that its meaning is not limited to the black theological movement beginning in the 1960s. In this chapter, I work out a definition of black theology as the interpretation of any religion (or religious beliefs), positively or negatively, in relation to blackness. The black theology emerging from the black theological movement of the 1960s fits the definition of black theology stated in this chapter. However, as I endeavor to show, this movement is unique in that it resulted in the rise of professional academic theologians for the interpretation of black theology. Prior to the contemporary black theological movement in seminaries, divinity schools, and departments of religion, even in predominately black schools, African Americans could not study and concentrate on African American religion as a legitimate academic subject area.[4] Academic black theology is not only the first sustained form of African American theology in institutions of higher learning but also the prevailing model of African American theology in these institutions. Chapter 1 relativizes academic black theology demonstrating

---

4. Charles S. Rooks, *Revolution in Zion: Reshaping African American Ministry, 1960–1974* (New York: Pilgrim Press, 1990), 121.

the origins, and therefore the legitimacy, of academic black theology in African American religious life and its place among competing, informal, unsystematic formulations of black theology in African American churches and communities.

Chapters 2, 3, and 4 examine the three methodological perspectives constituting the field of academic black theology. Chapter 2 examines the Black Hermeneutical School; chapter 3, the Black Philosophical School; and chapter 4, the Human Sciences School. The methodological perspective of each school becomes apparent in the identification of each school's representative thinkers and their views on the tasks, content, sources, norm, method, and goal of black theology. The table at the end of this preface shows the similarities and differences among the three schools of academic black theology and summarizes the content of chapters 2, 3, and 4.

This kind of comparative analysis — identifying and describing schools of thought according to how each school defines the tasks, content, sources, norms, method, and goal of black theology — is useful for three reasons. First, my aim is to show the distinct approaches to black theology, which this analytical method allows. Second, the structuring of systematic theology used here for a critical analysis of academic black theology makes the field intelligible to persons engaged in other fields of religious and theological study. Contemporary theologians commonly discuss systematic theology in terms of its tasks, content, sources, norm, and the like. An analysis of academic black theology in these terms establishes a bridge of communication between academic theologians and provides a basis for comparative studies between black theology and various other specialty areas in contemporary systematic theology.

Last, the structuring of systematic theology into the components of tasks, content, sources, and the like already occurs in academic black theology. In order to make "Christians, black and white, especially theologians and preachers, take black theology seriously,"[5] James Cone published the first two systematic works in black theology, *Black Theology and Black Power* (1969) and *A Black Theology of Liberation* (1970), using indiscriminately the theological structure and conceptual cate-

---

5. James H. Cone, *A Black Theology of Liberation,* Twentieth Anniversary Edition (Philadelphia: Lippincott, 1970; Maryknoll, N.Y.: Orbis Books, 1990), xi.

gories of Karl Barth, Paul Tillich, Dietrich Bonhoeffer, and Rudolf Bultmann for this purpose.[6] In *A Black Theology of Liberation, God of the Oppressed* (1975), and subsequent works, Cone constructs black theology through a unique and radical redefinition of the tasks, content, sources, norm, method, and goal of Christian theology. Other black theologians, such as Cecil Cone and Charles Long, criticized James Cone for his use of this rational structure in the construction of black theology. However, neither Long nor Cecil Cone has produced an alternative framework for interpreting black theology. Gayraud Wilmore and J. Deotis Roberts maintain that creation of an alternative structure is a challenging task that is better left to future scholars.[7] Roberts contends that creating such a structure could take a lifetime or longer.[8] Although suspicious of the structure currently used in academic black theology, Wilmore is content with it so long as the black experience remains the principal source and authority for reflection until someone produces an interpretive framework based on the oral tradition and literature of African Americans.[9] James Evans argues that precisely this emphasis on the black experience as source and authority allows black theology to achieve a revision of the theological tradition from whose tools it borrows.[10]

Many outstanding thinkers are contributing to the interpretation of African American religion. Since examining the works of them all is impossible, I use three criteria for selecting thinkers for this study. The first criterion is whether the thinker is ultimately concerned or committed to interpreting African American religion. This criterion broadens the term "theologian" to include systematic theologians, philosophers of religion, historians of religion, and other scholars with interests in interpreting religion. My first criterion for selection of thinkers finds support in Paul Tillich's definition of the "theologian." He says:

6. James H. Cone, *My Soul Looks Back* (Nashville: Abingdon Press, 1982; Maryknoll, N.Y.: Orbis Books, 1986), 82.
7. Gayraud S. Wilmore, *Black Religion and Black Radicalism: An Interpretation of the Religious History of Afro-American People,* 2d ed., revised and enlarged (Maryknoll, N.Y.: Orbis Books, 1983), 236–37; J. Deotis Roberts, *Black Theology Today: Liberation and Contextualization* (New York: Edwin Mellon Press, 1983), 26.
8. Roberts, *Black Theology Today,* 26.
9. Wilmore, *Black Religion and Black Radicalism,* 2d ed., 236–37.
10. James H. Evans, "Deconstructing the Tradition: Narrative Strategies in Nascent Black Theology," *Union Seminary Quarterly Review* 44 (1990): 116–17.

A person can be a theologian as long as he acknowledges the content of the theological circle as his ultimate concern. Whether this is true does not depend on his intellectual or moral or emotional state; it does not depend on the intensity and certitude of faith; it does not depend on the power of regeneration or the grade of sanctification. Rather it depends on his being ultimately concerned with the Christian message even if he is sometimes inclined to attack it or reject it.[11]

My second criterion for selecting thinkers is whether the individual demonstrates leadership and influence in the black theological movement. My third criterion is whether the individual has published major work(s) or made significant proposals that are crucial to defining a distinct methodological perspective. Based on these criteria, thinkers representing the Black Hermeneutical School are Katie Cannon, Albert Cleage, Cecil Cone, James Cone, Kelly Brown Douglas, James Evans, Jacquelyn Grant, Dwight Hopkins, Major Jones, Olin Moyd, J. Deotis Roberts, Delores Williams, and Gayraud Wilmore. Thinkers in the Black Philosophical School are William R. Jones, Anthony Pinn, Alice Walker, Cornel West, and Henry Young. Included in the Human Sciences School are Cheryl Townsend Gilkes, C. Eric Lincoln, Charles Long, Henry Mitchell, Charles Rooks, and Theophus Smith.

While employing the broadest possible definition of theologian in this study of academic black theology, I was compelled to exercise some restrictions on the concept of the theologian with respect to the Black Hermeneutical School. Several African American biblical scholars, ethicists, religious historians, pastoral theologians, and specialists in other theological disciplines are appropriating for their work themes and insights in black liberation theology and womanist theology as defined in the Black Hermeneutical School. Therefore, within the scope of this study, dealing with the views of all individuals from all theological disciplines utilizing the model of black theology found in the Black Hermeneutical School would be impossible. Because the majority of thinkers in academic black theology qualify for inclusion in the Black Hermeneutical School and in order to reduce this group to a manageable size, I exercised a bias in selecting mostly those thinkers who by

---

11. Paul Tillich, *Systematic Theology*, vol. 1: *Reason and Revelation, Being and God* (Chicago: University of Chicago Press, 1951), 10.

training or specialization regard themselves as professional systematic theologians.

The reader may notice that more men than women appear among this selection of thinkers. This lack of women's representation exposes the male dominance in academic black theology. Moreover, though womanist thought shares similar concerns with black theology and white feminist theology, black womanists do not regard their work as an appendage to either of the two. Womanists assert their freedom to determine their own academic enterprise, to think and act independently of white and black male and white female theologians. Nonetheless, I have incorporated elements of womanist thought into each chapter in order to give more definition to the methodological perspective examined therein.

The reader must not assume that rigid lines separate black theologians. A thinker's principal work within one perspective does not bar him or her from interest and participation in the activity most peculiar to another perspective. For example, J. Deotis Roberts operates principally within the Black Hermeneutical School, but he has formal training and a continuing interest in philosophy — just as do other thinkers in the Black Philosophical School. Roberts describes himself as a philosophical theologian, someone committed to the Christian faith and who seeks to answer the questions that philosophy poses for religious faith. For another example, while stressing knowledge with broad applications as the goal of black theology, Charles Rooks is involved in educational reforms aimed at strengthening the role of churches in the liberation of African American communities. In still another example, although Cornel West is best classified with thinkers in the Black Philosophical School, he does not view his work as abstract philosophical analysis but rather as a form of cultural criticism that is compatible with the concept of cultural studies emphasized in the Human Sciences School. Anthony Pinn is capable of association with thinkers in the Black Philosophical School because of his use of humanism but he pursues the study of African American religion within a religious studies context, as does Theophus Smith in the Human Sciences School. In the Black Hermeneutical School, Olin Moyd's concept of redemption is similar to the concept of empowerment found in the Human Sciences School. Though not included in this study, the ethicist Cheryl Sanders could be classified among thinkers in the Black Hermeneutical School. She actually uses, like thinkers in the Human Sciences School, the term "empowerment" to identify the content of black theology.

The unequal lengths of chapters 2, 3, and 4 warrant an explanation. Because the Black Hermeneutical School is the largest and most prolific of the three schools of academic black theology, I felt no compulsion to weary readers already familiar with this school of thought. Therefore, I dealt with the thinkers and literature in the Black Hermeneutical School that adequately demonstrate its unique methodological perspective. Chapter 4, which examines the Human Sciences School, is the shortest of the three because thinkers in the Human Sciences School are not prolific writers in systematic theology. Chapter 3 is the longest chapter. My description of the Black Philosophical School's norm may prove to be challenging reading. My aim is to make the reader aware of the positions and subtleties of argument in the Black Philosophical School, which like the Human Sciences School receives little attention or due regard as a legitimate approach to black theology.

In the concluding chapter, I stress what I do here in this preface: diversity. The schools of thought described in this book are well established and will continue to play important roles in the field of African American theology. These frameworks of interpretation will continue to form a basis for research, teaching, and publication, but I still sense new possibilities. I identify seven areas of new and/or continuing development in African American theology in addition to the summary of the three schools shown in the following table.

•

Many persons and institutions helped me at various stages in the research for and writing of this book. I am thankful to them. The book began with my dissertation research at Vanderbilt University. I am especially grateful to Professors Victor Anderson and Peter C. Hodgson for their critical reading of the dissertation. Other dissertation committee members to whom I am thankful are Professors Lewis V. Baldwin, Michael P. Hodges, and Sallie McFague. Both the dissertation and this book were enhanced by a course in black theology that I taught twice at Memphis Theological Seminary. My thoughts on black theology were refined by the probing questions and provocative reflections of students taking the course. In appreciation to these students, I list their names here: Jimmy Barnes, Don Fuller, Brenda Ivy, Paul Hillard, Andre Johnson, Verlena Johnson, Eddie Jones, Sammie Listenbee, Gloria McKinney, Jacqueline Pryer, William Reynolds, Spencer Stoker, Pearly Stone, William Warr, and David Wright. I appreciate the help of librarians at Vanderbilt University, Memphis Theological Seminary, Christian Brothers University, and the University of Memphis. The ease with which the book can be read is due to the excellent editorial work of George Graham and Bob Land at The Pilgrim Press. I owe a special word of thanks to Professor William R. Jones. In spite of very serious illness, he talked with me at length about his method of internal criticism, which he describes in the 1998 revised edition of *Is God a White Racist?*

# Three Schools of Academic Black Theology

|  | Black Hermeneutical | Black Philosophical | Human Sciences |
|---|---|---|---|
| *Thinkers* | Katie Cannon, Albert Cleage, Cecil Cone, James Cone, Kelly Brown Douglas, James Evans, Jacquelyn Grant, Dwight Hopkins, Major Jones, Olin Moyd, J. Deotis Roberts, Delores Williams, Gayraud Wilmore | William R. Jones, Anthony Pinn, Alice Walker, Cornel West, Henry Young | Cheryl Townsend Gilkes, C. Eric Lincoln, Charles Long, Henry Mitchell, Charles Rooks, Theophus Smith |
| *Tasks* | Description, analysis, evaluation, explanation, construction, and revision (also called *deconstruction*) | Description, analysis, evaluation, explanation, construction, and revision (also called *gnosiological conversion*) | Description, analysis, evaluation, explanation, revision (also called *deconstruction*), and construction (when approached inductively) |
| *Content* | Liberation, as defined by biblical conceptions of God's liberating activity and black folk stories on freedom | Liberation, as defined by social and political philosophy, which may or may not be compatible with biblical story and black story | Empowerment: power to endure, re-vision, transform, and overcome various conditions of human life |
| *Sources* | Revelation; Bible; Black experience, spirituality, history, and culture; and Reason (i.e., as expressed in intellectual sources external to the community of faith and disciplines/subject areas external to theology) when compatible with Revelation | Reason (i.e., as expressed in philosophical traditions such as humanism, process metaphysics, and disciplines/subject areas external to theology or faith community); Black experience, history, culture, etc.; and traditional theological sources like the Bible, Christian tradition, etc., when compatible with Reason | Black religion and culture, both understood as a complex system of thought and action that orients persons to the ultimate significance of their place in the world; and any sources (internal or external to black religion) relevant to the interpretation of black religion as it "appears" rather than as a transcendent, ahistorical reality |
| *Norm* | Nonfoundationalist (i.e., biblical, communal, and personal) conceptions of Christian faith centered in Jesus Christ as the black Messiah and leading to the privileging of blackness and liberation | Foundationalist (i.e., humanist) conceptions of Christian faith, which do not privilege blackness but do privilege liberation; philosophical and academic canons of truth and rationality | Foundationalist (i.e., phenomenological) conceptions of religion, which acknowledge but do not privilege blackness and liberation; academic canons of truth and rationality |
| *Method* | Hermeneutics: methods such as biblical and philosophical hermeneutics, correlation, and narrative criticism | Philosophical analysis, empirical analysis, logical argument, biblical and philosophical hermeneutics | Hermeneutics and social science methodologies: case study analysis, heuristic categories, etc. |
| *Goal* | Moral and ethical action leading to liberation | Moral and ethical action leading to liberation | Knowledge for multiple purposes |

# CHAPTER ONE

# A Genealogy of Black Theology

**M**ORE THAN ANY PIONEER of the black theological movement of the 1960s, Gayraud S. Wilmore understands the difficulty of assigning a specific origin to black theology. He says:

> The etiology of Black Theology is difficult. It is the intellectual reflex of the Black religious community to oppression, and all of the subtleties and complexities of White racism are involved. It has been an interpretation of the Christian religion for degraded and subordinated Blacks that surfaced from time to time throughout the history of the race in the New World. But the inability of White theologians to articulate an American perspective of the Christian faith that would encompass the distinctive perceptions of Black Christians and the failure of White church leaders to assimilate Black churchmen within the policy-making and programmatic structures of the establishment with effective power gave rise to Black Theology's radical revisitation in the mid-1960s.[1]

According to Wilmore, black theology did not begin in the 1960s. He contends that "this way of doing theology is at least as old as the Atlantic slave trade, if not older."[2] This chapter makes a suggestive charting of black theology in the United States, offering an explanation of what black theology is, how it emerged, and the practice of black

---

1. Gayraud S. Wilmore, Introduction to Part II: The Attack on White Religion, in *Black Theology: A Documentary History, 1966–1979*, ed. James H. Cone and Gayraud S. Wilmore (Maryknoll, N.Y.: Orbis Books, 1979), 72.
2. Gayraud S. Wilmore, "Pastoral Ministry in the Origin and Development of Black Theology," in *Black Theology: A Documentary History, Volume Two: 1980–1992*, ed. James H. Cone and Gayraud S. Wilmore (Maryknoll, N.Y.: Orbis Books, 1993), 117.

theology prior to and after the academic turn of black theology in the 1960s.[3]

## STAGES IN THE DEVELOPMENT OF BLACK THEOLOGY

Intermittently but over centuries, black theology has interpreted Christianity in such as way as to recover from racist distortion Christianity's transformative message. As I understand Wilmore, he seems to say that the severity of race relations in the 1960s among black and white Christians provoked black theology's transition from a sporadic intellectual enterprise to an incessant discipline claiming to be a legitimate form of Christian theology. Wilmore's grand view of black theology does not make him oblivious to the development of contemporary black theology. As head of the Theological Commission of the National Conference of Black Churchmen (NCBC) and key participant in nearly all of the early dialogues on issues in black theology, Wilmore is precise and meticulous in his interpretation of the contemporary black theological movement. He sees contemporary black theology evolving over a span of three distinct stages.[4]

The first stage is the emergence of black theology from the civil rights and black power movements. Most notable in the civil rights movement was Martin Luther King Jr.'s interpretation of the African American struggle for civil rights within the framework of Christianity. King contended that civil rights ideals and intended reforms, focusing on social justice and racial integration, are compatible with Christianity. King's most succinct and classic statement on the Christian principles underlying the civil rights movement is his "Letter from Birmingham City Jail."[5] The letter was written in response to leading white clergy

3. For more detailed histories of black theology, the reader may consult James H. Cone's *For My People* (1984), Gayraud S. Wilmore's *Black Religion and Black Radicalism* (1983), and Mark L. Chapman's *Christianity on Trial* (1996). A two-volume anthology that Cone and Wilmore co-edited under the title of *Black Theology: A Documentary History* covers the years 1966 through 1992.

4. Gayraud S. Wilmore, General Introduction to *Black Theology: A Documentary History, 1966–1979*, ed. Cone and Wilmore, 4–9; James H. Cone, *For My People: Black Theology and the Black Church* (Maryknoll, N.Y.: Orbis Books, 1984), 24–28.

5. Martin Luther King Jr., "Letter from Birmingham City Jail," in *A Testament of Hope: The Essential Writings of Martin Luther King Jr.*, ed. James M. Washington (San Francisco: Harper & Row, 1986), 289–302.

who condemned the civil rights movement in Birmingham.[6] The gist of the letter is that professing Christians, white as well as black, had a moral obligation to support the civil rights movement. The movement represented an opportunity for Christians to live out constructively their faith in Christ. Inspired by King's example, radical clergy of the NCBC — such as Metz Rollins, Leon Watts, Will Herzfeld, Lawrence Lucas, Herbert Bell Shaw, M. L. Wilson, and Albert B. Cleage — also sought to interpret Christianity in relation to the African American struggle for civil liberty. However, these radical clergy departed from King in their interpretation of Christianity in light of the black power movement.

King agreed with the black power movement's much needed call to African Americans to amass political and economic strength for the purpose of exercising greater leverage in achieving social change. Nonetheless, he saw the movement as being basically a "nihilistic philosophy" born out of the conviction that American society is so corrupt that African Americans cannot achieve change through existing social institutions.[7] Radical black clergy issued a statement in defense of the black power movement and its compatibility with Christian faith.[8] In the statement, they contend that the concept of power is not antithetical to Christian faith but for Christian people an item of concern since the Protestant Reformation. The radical black clergy claim that at the heart of the Reformation is the belief that humans do not have the same degree of moral integrity as God with respect to possessing tremendous power and simultaneously acting responsibly in the use of that power. Humans act immorally and most brutally against one another when power is concentrated in the hands of a few. While these clergy accept racial reconciliation as the goal of the black liberation struggle, they caution against black people's integration with whites

---

6. The public statement directed in criticism of Martin Luther King Jr. that occasioned his famous letter was signed by C. C. J. Carpenter (Bishop of Alabama), Joseph A. Durick (Auxiliary Bishop, Diocese of Mobile-Birmingham), Rabbi Milton L. Grafman (Temple Emanu-El, Birmingham, Alabama), Paul Hardin (Bishop, Alabama-West Florida Conference of Methodist Church), Nolan B. Harmon (Bishop, North Alabama Conference of Methodist Church), George M. Murray (Bishop Co-adjutor, Episcopal Diocese of Alabama), Edward V. Ramage (Moderator, Synod of the Alabama Presbyterian Church, U.S.A.), and Earl Stallings (Pastor, First Baptist Church, Birmingham, Alabama).

7. Martin Luther King Jr., *Where Do We Go from Here?: Chaos or Community,* in *A Testament of Hope,* ed. Washington, 582–83.

8. Statement by the National Committee of Negro Churchmen (July 31, 1966), in *Black Theology: A Documentary History, 1966–1979,* ed. Cone and Wilmore, 23–30.

from a position of disadvantage. They claim that black power — black racial unity and cooperation, the amassing of black people's resources, the development of black institutions and culture — enables blacks to participate as equals with whites and other ethnic groups in the creation of a just social order in the United States.

The second stage of black theology is its entry into academic settings. The earliest discussions on black theology occurred in black ecumenical church settings. According to Wilmore, this second stage begins with the participation in the NCBC's Theological Commission of black seminary professors such as James H. Cone, Major Jones, J. Deotis Roberts, and Preston Williams. With the gradual demise of the NCBC and increasing growth in professional forums for black seminary professors, black theology tackles concerns rarely, if ever, expressed in church settings. Wilmore notes that black seminary professors in this second stage tend to focus on issues in the definition and methodology of black theology, more so than did the radical black clergy during stage one. James Cone's *Black Theology and Black Power* (1969) and *A Black Theology of Liberation* (1970), the first systematic works produced in the contemporary black theological movement, led the way for works of other seminary professors. In response to Cone, Roberts wrote *Liberation and Reconciliation* (1971); Major Jones, *Black Awareness* (1971); Wilmore, *Black Religion and Black Radicalism* (1973); William Jones, *Is God a White Racist?* (1973); and Cecil Cone, *Identity Crisis in Black Theology* (1975). The debates underlying these publications centered on three issues: (1) the meaning of black liberation, its relation to racial reconciliation, and the place, if any, of violence in the struggle for liberation; (2) the nature of black religion and its relation to black theology as the latter's principal subject matter; and (3) the plausibility of black liberation theism, that is, belief in God's solidarity with oppressed blacks, in the face of their continued suffering and the absence of compelling empirical evidence in support of divine liberating activity.[9]

The third stage of black theology is its return to the black church and focus on global issues in relationship to African American communities. The involvement of professional black theologians in the

---

9. James H. Cone, "An Interpretation of the Debate among Black Theologians," Epilogue to *Black Theology: A Documentary History, 1966–1979*, ed. Cone and Wilmore, 612.

"Theology in the Americas Projects," lasting from 1975 to 1980, broadened the field of academic black theology to include discussions on gender and sexuality; environmental devastation; and the relationship between black theology, other liberation theologies, and Marxist critiques of American capitalism. Thus, a broader range of issues and greater relevance to life beyond institutions of higher learning characterizes the third stage of black theology.

## CONTEMPORARY CONCEPTIONS OF BLACK THEOLOGY

To Wilmore's three-stage historical analysis, Dwight Hopkins adds a fourth and present stage that began in the mid-1980s,[10] led by what he calls a "second generation" of scholars and pastors. The focus of these scholars and clergy is on strengthening ties between scholarship, ministry, and social activism. This second generation includes womanist thinkers who are not only interpreting African American women's experiences but also seeking a holistic perspective that deals adequately with issues pertaining to race, class, gender, sexual orientation, and ecology. According to Hopkins, first-generation thinkers, all male, include Albert Cleage, Cecil Cone, James Cone, Charles Copher, Vincent Harding, Major Jones, William R. Jones, Carlton Lee, Charles Long, Henry Mitchell, J. Deotis Roberts, Charles Shelby Rooks, Joseph Washington, Preston Williams, and Gayraud Wilmore.[11] In contrast to "first generation" or "pioneer" thinkers in the first three stages of black theology, the second generation explores black theology from any and all aspects of African American life and culture — forming new academic guilds, focusing research on previously neglected or unutilized primary sources, and developing models of organic relation for scholars' involvement in African American churches and communities.

Hopkins's use of the term "second generation" is misleading. The term implies that persons writing in black theology in the late '60s to mid-'80s are being replaced or that their work lacks equal or greater

---

10. Dwight N. Hopkins, *Introducing Black Theology of Liberation* (Maryknoll, N.Y.: Orbis Books, 1999), 10–12.

11. Ibid., 53, 66, 210–11 n. 1.

importance with respect to current publications in the field. The term "second generation" also implies a third and subsequent generations. The use of numerical sequence in order to describe change within the field of black theology commits us to the notion of multiple generations. If the first generation is followed by a second, what is there to keep the second from being followed by a third, fourth, and so on? Will latter generations be better than previous generations? In the black theological movement, as is true throughout the contemporary black studies movement, most scholars are self-taught. Black studies courses are increasingly offered in institutions of higher learning, but few comprehensive graduate-level programs exist for study and research in African American life and culture. James Cone admits that he and other persons were self-taught black theologians, many lacking terminal degrees in theology and almost all lacking formal preparation for doing black theology.[12] Today more, but still small numbers of, persons with proper formal education are teaching and performing research in black studies. Cone is justified, however, in maintaining that "smarter" and more knowledgeable does not mean necessarily "better" or more committed.[13]

Wilmore's history of contemporary black theology is neither exhaustive nor the only proposed history of contemporary black theology. James Cone and Anthony Pinn have proposed histories that differ from Wilmore's history of black theology. On the one hand, Cone claims — and Wilmore makes no argument against him — that the origin of contemporary black theology has three major contexts: the civil rights movement, the publication of Joseph Washington's controversial book *Black Religion* (1964), and the black power movement.[14] According to Cone, these three contexts serve as the initial impetus for contemporary black theology which, as he agrees with Wilmore, was at first restricted to radical black clergy in ecumenical church settings, then entered and flourished in academic settings, and now seeks to reenter and gain a wider audience in African American churches.

Anthony Pinn offers five historical phases of black theology. In his view, black theology is progressive and cumulative, starting well before

---

12. James H. Cone, General Introduction to *Black Theology: A Documentary History, Volume 2: 1980–1992*, ed. Cone and Wilmore, 2.
13. Ibid., 9–10.
14. Cone, *For My People*, 5–28.

the twentieth century and moving on to a second phase of intellectualizing during the civil rights movement. Its third phase is globalization through cross-cultural dialogue, while the fourth phase is one of inclusion of previously excluded voices through provocative discussions on gender and sexuality. A fifth and present phase of black theology is its expanding range and scope of black theological sources for the interpretation of the black experience.[15]

Notwithstanding Cone's and Pinn's accounts of black theology, Wilmore's historiography of the contemporary black theology movement is most noteworthy. While Wilmore gives special attention to the origin and progressive development of contemporary black theology, he recognizes that black theology in general is not restricted to circumstances unique to the 1960s. Wilmore does not view contemporary black theology as the culmination or exemplary expression of black religious thought. According to him, black theology is typical of a longstanding practice of African Americans to interpret religion in light of their economic, social, and political condition. Moreover, the desired end of this longstanding practice is economic, social, cultural, and political transformation.[16]

Wilmore holds that radicalism — the quest for economic, social, and political change — is not limited to any particular religion. Since the early debates of contemporary black theology, he has maintained that the essential radical quality of African American religion is not reducible to Christianity.[17] Indeed, "African American religious life has never been confined solely to the Christian tradition. It has found expression in Islam, Judaism, Hinduism, Vodun, New Thought, and many other religious modalities, some created de novo."[18] Wilmore is careful not to assert that African American religion is reducible to radicalism. He acknowledges that African American religion is characterized by several tendencies. However, his opinion is that radicalism

---

15. Anthony B. Pinn, *Why Lord? Suffering and Evil in Black Theology* (New York: Continuum, 1995), 18.

16. Gayraud S. Wilmore, "A Revolution Unfulfilled, but Not Invalidated," in Cone, *A Black Theology of Liberation,* Twentieth Anniversary Edition, 147.

17. Cone, "An Interpretation of the Debate among Black Theologians," Epilogue to *Black Theology: A Documentary History, 1966–1979,* ed. Cone and Wilmore, 617.

18. Larry G. Murphy, "Religion in the African American Community," in *Encyclopedia of African American Religions,* ed. Larry G. Murphy, J. Gordon Melton, and Gary L. Ward (New York: Garland Publishing, 1993), xxxii.

is "the most distinctive, persistent, and valuable part of the religious heritage of African Americans in the United States."[19]

William R. Jones would go further to suggest that the radical tendency in African American religion, as pointed out by Wilmore, does not necessarily involve a positive affirmation of the religion under interpretation. According to Jones, both positive and negative interpretations of a religion have a place in the field of African American religious and theological studies.[20] For Jones, serious consideration of multiple frameworks of belief (beliefs of a religion as well as beliefs in opposition to a religion) is necessary in the study of black theology.

In light of the preceding discussion on the relationship of black theology to African American religion and on the origins of black theology itself, I shall offer a working definition of black theology. I define "black theology" as the interpretation, positive or negative, of any religion (or religious beliefs) in relation to the experience of blackness. Blackness may be, and more often is, characterized by experiences of oppression, humiliation, discrimination, political disenfranchisement, economic injustice, and so on. When these negative aspects of black people's experience are of chief concern, black theology takes on a liberation orientation with the aim of transforming the conditions that adversely affect black people's lives. However, blackness may also refer to those positive aspects, what James Cone calls the "beauty and joy," of African American life that are expressive of deeply held values and mores that enable African Americans' fulfillment as human beings.[21]

Therefore, besides liberation, black theology may emphasize themes such as empowerment, fulfillment, and self-understanding as an identifiable ethnic group. Quoting Geddes Hanson of Princeton, Major Jones agrees with his claim that "Black Theology ... is a conscious effort to relate the experiences of American Blackness to the corpus of Christian theology."[22] But as mentioned earlier in this chapter, the religious life of African Americans is not limited to Christianity or

---

19. Wilmore, "A Revolution Unfulfilled," in Cone, *A Black Theology of Liberation,* Twentieth Anniversary Edition, 147.

20. William R. Jones, "Religious Humanism: Its Problems and Prospects in Black Religion and Culture," *Journal of the Interdenominational Theological Center* 7 (spring 1980): 176.

21. James H. Cone, *God of the Oppressed* (San Francisco: Harper & Row, Seabury Press, 1975), 2.

22. Major J. Jones, *Black Awareness: A Theology of Hope* (Nashville: Abingdon Press, 1971), 12.

Christian thought. Black theology is a widespread cultural phenom-enon that finds expression in various African American intellectual and religious traditions. After having defined black theology in the above way, the genealogy of this chapter takes up the question of "What historic and cultural conditions gave rise to black theology?"

## ROOTS IN SLAVERY AND RESISTANCE

Whereas Wilmore's approach is general, offering little detail about the emergence of black theology in the American system of chattel slavery, religious historians such as Thomas L. Webber and Albert J. Raboteau and ethicist Riggins R. Earl offer insights on how black theology could have emerged during this period of American history. According to Webber and Raboteau, black theology emerges in the resistance of African slaves to the identity assigned to them by their oppressors, who used Christianity as a sanction for slavery. In his study of the American slave system, Webber observes that slaves early on discerned that the preaching of their captors was a distortion of Christianity. According to Webber, in slave communities the cultural theme existed that "true Christianity" is distinct from "slaveholding religion."[23] Webber says:

> Slaves were taught that it was God's design, as decreed by the Holy Scriptures, that they, as the sons and daughters of Ham, be servants of whites into eternity. The life of a hewer of wood and carrier of water was not to be thought of as a curse, however. Rather it was to be recognized as a blessing in disguise; God's means of providing a road to salvation for the pagan African.[24]

After witnessing and experiencing the worst of abuses, those slaves who did convert to Christianity reached the conclusion that the piety of slaveholders was a contrived interpretation of Christianity designed for the continued oppression of nonwhite people. Slaves may have thought this way as early as the fifteenth century, if in fact black theology is wedded to slaves' reactions to the piety of slaveholders. Raboteau finds in his study of slave religion a fifteenth-century docu-ment written by Gomes Eannes De Azurara who justifies the brutality

---

23. Thomas L. Webber, *Deep Like the Rivers: Education in the Slave Quarter Community, 1831–1865* (New York: W. W. Norton, 1978), 80–81.

24. Ibid., 49.

of the Portuguese slavers as a necessary, instrumental evil for freeing the souls of Africans from paganism.[25]

Actually, Christianity is subject to interpretation in a variety of ways. However, the potential of a religion is not restricted to any present or past forms of expression. The slaves' cultural theme of true Christianity versus slaveholding religion and identification of only their interpretation of Christianity as true denied any validity to the masters' interpretation of Christian faith. For slaves to have attributed legitimacy to both their and the masters' interpretations would give no absolute value to freedom and therefore frustrate their aspirations for emancipation.

According to Riggins Earl, the crisis-ridden status of Africans in the New World is explainable within the context of the body-soul problem. The person or self in Western thought is considered to be principally a union of body and soul, two distinct realities that make up each person. The body is the material composition, physical aspect, and biological makeup of the person. The soul is the immaterial, spiritual, rational aspects of the person. The soul is thought to be eternal, or at the very least, something that persists over time and not subject to decay like the body. Body and soul are usually related hierarchically. The soul is usually valued over the body.

The dualism of body and soul finds unique and tragic expression in the experience of African slaves. Earl says that blacks were viewed by their oppressors as being either "soulless bodies" or "bodiless souls."[26] Earl contends that these misinterpretations of the slave's anthropological nature constitute the core theological and ethical problem of American slavery.[27] As bodiless souls, blacks were, to a limited degree, regarded as human. Whites' acknowledgment of blacks as having souls meant that whites recognized blacks as possessing a valued aspect of personhood. However, the humanity recognized and affirmed in blacks' souls was not affirmed in their bodily, physical existence. Regarding blacks as bodiless souls, whites were compelled to make slavery more humane. Efforts were made at evangelizing slaves. Concerned

25. Albert J. Raboteau, *Slave Religion: The "Invisible Institution" in the Antebellum South* (New York: Oxford University Press, 1978), 96.

26. Riggins R. Earl Jr., *Dark Symbols, Obscure Signs: God, Self, and Community in the Slave Mind* (Maryknoll, N.Y.: Orbis Books, 1993), 5.

27. Ibid.

clergy and laity emphasized the obligations of masters to provide food, clothing, housing, medical care, sufficient periods of rest, and so forth for their slaves who were, in turn, required to submit and obey.[28]

As soulless bodies, the humanity of blacks was denied altogether. Blacks were seen as bodies only, as physical machines for the production of wealth. Blacks were thought to be subhuman and on the level of beasts. Those whites who viewed blacks in this way had no sense of moral responsibility toward them or even toward God for their mistreatment of blacks.

Frederick Douglass's recollection of his experiences of slavery illustrates whites' conceptions of black slaves as bodiless souls and soulless bodies. Douglass states that William Freeland was the best master that he had ever had, until that time when, according to Douglass, he became his own master.[29] Freeland considered Douglass and other slaves to be bodiless souls. According to Douglass, Freeland exhibited a sense of morality, reverence for justice, and respect for humanity, including that of the slaves.[30] Freeland worked his slaves hard but always made sure that they were well clothed, fed, rested, and had sufficient tools with which to work.

Douglass reports that the worst experiences of slaves resulted from whites who viewed slaves as a soulless bodies. These whites, whom Douglass said were the greatest professors of religion, either did not think that blacks had souls or, if they did think that blacks had souls, they believed that blacks had a limited capacity for salvation. The sabotage of a Sabbath school that Douglass set up illustrates the terrible consequences of whites' perceptions of blacks as soulless bodies. Douglass conducted this Sabbath school for the purpose of teaching his fellow slaves, and some free blacks, the basics of reading and writing as well as the literature of the Bible. Upon learning of its existence, after it had operated in secrecy for close to one year, white church members burst into Douglass's Sabbath school, beating several black slaves and daring them to ever meet again.[31]

---

28. Raboteau, *Slave Religion*, 152ff.
29. Frederick Douglass, *Narrative of the Life of Frederick Douglass, An American Slave* (1845; reprinted, New York: Signet Books, 1968), 90.
30. Ibid., 86.
31. Ibid., 89.

Whether blacks were viewed as bodiless souls or soulless bodies, the dual aspects of personhood were not simultaneously accorded to blacks. If looked upon as bodiless souls, then only the soul was affirmed while the body was denied the privilege of freedom. If looked upon as soulless bodies, then only the body was affirmed, and then only for its usefulness in producing wealth for the slaveholder.

According to Earl, black liberation thought — that is, black theology — begins with the slave's assertion, "I am my body."[32] In other words, slaves were saying: "The humanity that is affirmed in my soul must also be affirmed in my body." The slaves were in effect redefining blackness. In discarding the negative images of blackness that whites first ascribed to them, slaves were reworking the concept of blackness to achieve a positive self-identity. At the same time that they were re-defining blackness, slaves were restructuring its relation to Christianity. According to Earl, this redefinition of black identity and its subsequent renegotiation to Christianity is noticeably present in slaves' conversion accounts, spirituals, personal narratives, and folk tales.[33]

Blackness was not defined definitively, once and for all, in the slave period. For subsequent generations of African Americans, the task of defining blackness has involved the challenge of resolving various dichotomies centering on questions of whether blacks are essentially African or fully American, privileged or oppressed, citizens or non-citizens, and so forth. W. E. B. Du Bois asked the question: "What, after all am I? Am I an American or am I a Negro? Can I be both?"[34] Du Bois was aware of the guarantees of citizenship accorded to blacks by the Thirteenth, Fourteenth, and Fifteenth Amendments to the Constitution of the United States, but his experience of segregation taught him that enforcement of this legislation was tenuous. Du Bois knew that he was a citizen but his experience did not make him feel like a citizen. Aware of his commonality with other Americans, he still realized that his African ancestry and cultural affinities set him apart from other Americans. Du Bois's intention was to achieve a coherent, positive self-identity and group solidarity, very much like that of African

---

32. Earl, *Dark Symbols, Obscure Signs,* 105, 174–75.
33. Ibid., 1, 46, 70, 104, 131.
34. W. E. B. Du Bois, "Conservation of the Races," cited in James H. Cone, *Martin and Malcolm and America: A Dream or a Nightmare?* (Maryknoll, N.Y.: Orbis Books, 1991), 3.

slaves striving to bring together the dual aspects of their personhood into a unity worthy of affirmation.

Du Bois contended that the principal crisis that troubles African Americans is that of a "double consciousness." This double consciousness leads to a peculiar sensation of "twoness — an American, a Negro; two souls, two thoughts, two unreconciled strivings, two warring ideals in one dark body."[35] According to Du Bois, the history of blacks in America is fraught with images that are not always of their own making. Their goal then becomes to reconcile conflicting images into "a better and truer self."[36]

The ongoing task of identity formation among African Americans implies that black theology must be ongoing as well. If black theology, as defined earlier in this chapter, is the positive or negative interpretation of any religion (or religious beliefs) in relation to the experience of blackness, then the redefinition and renegotiation of black identity, if nothing else, will warrant continuing the practice of black theology. As long as race and religion circumscribe American reality, black theology will continue, with relevance to the lives of millions of Americans.

## BLACK THEOLOGY PRIOR TO THE 1960s

The case has been well made that the practice of black theology existed long before the 1960s. Even without knowledge of the tragic formulation of the body-soul problem in American slavery, one can look elsewhere for evidence of the practice of black theology before the 1960s. For instance, the lengthy history and expression of black theology is evident in the black sources used and appealed to by contemporary academic black theologians in their constructive theologies.

African American religious historiography has grown considerably. In a 1994 article in *Religious Studies Review*, Michael W. Harris states that the field has expanded exponentially each decade since the 1920s.[37] In the 1980s alone, fifty-six studies in African American religious his-

---

35. W. E. B. Du Bois, *The Souls of Black Folk* (1903; reprinted, Greenwich, Conn.: Fawcett Publications, 1961), 17.

36. Ibid.

37. Michael W. Harris, "African American Religious History in the 1980s: A Critical Review," *Religious Studies Review* 20, no. 4 (October 1994): 264.

tory were published. According to Harris, this number is more than the total amount of monographs published between 1920 and 1980.

The increasing research and publication in the field of African American religious history has resulted in greater awareness of the existence of primary source materials. Black theologians along with other scholars in African American religious studies are turning more to the sermons, songs, prayers, conversion narratives, religious testimony, slave interviews, folklore, poetry, fiction, church publications and records, manuscripts, oral histories, newspapers, letters, speeches, diaries, artifacts, autobiographies, and public documents discovered in historical research. Though black sources have still to be fully tapped and exhausted, Ethel L. Williams and Clifton F. Brown's compilation of *The Howard University Bibliography of African and Afro-American Religious History* (1977) is a pioneering work that remains a chief reference tool for identifying many of these sources and the special collections and libraries where they are held.

After the publication of *Black Theology and Black Power* (1969) and *A Black Theology of Liberation* (1970), James Cone met with criticism from Cecil Cone and Gayraud Wilmore, among other critics, who charged him with basing black theology on white Western theology and the contingent politics of the black power movement.[38] In *A Black Theology of Liberation,* Cone identifies black experience, black history, and black culture as sources for black theology.[39] However, not until Wilmore and Cecil Cone's criticisms does James Cone specify in his book *God of the Oppressed* (1975) that black experience, black history, and black culture are evident in particular sources such as sermons, prayers, songs, folklore, poetry, and fiction.[40]

James Cone's turn to black sources, and that of other black theologians persuaded of the need to incorporate black sources into their theological constructions, may be interpreted as a move toward legitimation.[41] Black sources are seldom treated in a historical-critical fashion that distinguishes these sources from the theological construc-

---

38. Cone, "An Interpretation of the Debate among Black Theologians," Epilogue to *Black Theology: A Documentary History, 1966–1979,* ed. Cone and Wilmore, 617.

39. Cone, *A Black Theology of Liberation,* Twentieth Anniversary Edition, 23–29.

40. Cone, *God of the Oppressed,* 17–30.

41. Victor Anderson, *Beyond Ontological Blackness: An Essay on African American Religious and Cultural Criticism* (New York: Continuum, 1995), 93, 99, 109–10.

tions produced by using them.[42] The sources are not scrutinized or interrogated; they are used instead to defend theological assertions. J. Deotis Roberts noted very early into the turn to black sources that their retrieval and use did not result in substantial change in black constructive theologies. Commenting on Cone's turn to black sources, Roberts says:

> Cone,...in his research into black sources, seems to impose ready-made structures of thought upon new materials and new experiences. He does not learn from these. His insights seem static. He always seems to find what he is seeking. For this reason, one does not find the freshness and evidence of growth one expects in a new book from his pen.[43]

Roberts seems to think that Cone uses black sources in a proof-texting fashion to confirm the claims that he has made already. Roberts assumes that a fair reading of previously neglected sources ought to have resulted in some modification of Cone's earliest attempts at the systematic construction of black theology.

Contemporary academic black theologians and their readers tend not to be aware of the diversity of expression and alternative strategies for liberation found in black sources. Academic black theology's distortion of black sources is implied in C. Eric Lincoln and Lawrence H. Mamiya's recent survey of black clergy and black churches. Lincoln and Mamiya point out that the militant and revolution-oriented constructive theologies of academic black theologians stand in stark contrast to older and more widely accepted conceptions of black liberation that stress the virtues of freedom, independence, economic uplift, and self-help.[44] Based upon Lincoln and Mamiya's findings, black theology splinters into multiple liberation traditions, not all of which are necessarily contradictory but each of which is certainly capable of separate development. J. Deotis Roberts's lament over the turn to and exclusive preoccupation with black sources is not hard to understand. Academic black theology's turn to black sources does not reflect the rich diversity of religious opinion in these sources. No tendency of any kind, how-

---

42. Ibid., 94–98.
43. Roberts, *Black Theology Today*, 42–43.
44. C. Eric Lincoln and Lawrence H. Mamiya, *The Black Church in the African American Experience* (Durham, N.C.: Duke University Press, 1990), 177–78, 181–83.

ever, in black theology was systematized until such deliberate efforts were made to construct systematic theologies from a black perspective starting in the 1960s.

## THE ACADEMIC TURN OF BLACK THEOLOGY

Prior to 1964, black theology was relatively unsystematized in whatever form it was expressed. This new attempt to construct systematic theologies from a black perspective I term the "academic turn" of black theology. The term "academic turn" should not be taken to mean that no scholarly works by African American religionists were produced before 1964. W. E. B. Du Bois's *The Souls of Black Folk* (1903) and *The Negro Church* (1903), Carter G. Woodson's *History of the Negro Church* (1921), Benjamin E. Mays's *The Negro's God* (1938), Howard Thurman's *Deep River* (1945) and *The Negro Spiritual Speaks of Life and Death* (1947), Ruby F. Johnston's *The Development of Negro Religion* (1954) and *The Religion of Negro Protestants* (1956), to name a few works, attest to the presence of scholarly interest in the study and interpretation of African American religion well before the 1960s. The academic turn is a momentous step toward professionalism in black theology. A lingering consequence of the black theological movement of the 1960s is the creation of an academic subject area that has recognized experts, leading thinkers, and authorities. Black theology is not merely a distinctive brand of religious thought existing in African American churches and communities, but it is also now a recognized area of study in institutions of higher learning. Several factors contributed to this state of affairs.

In 1964, Joseph Washington published his book *Black Religion*. Washington claimed that black churches really are not Christian churches but are instead political associations and therefore devoid of any theology. For Washington, the internal norm of Christianity is faith expressed in the form of theology. According to Washington, blacks have a religion that is a partial view of Christianity distorted by a preoccupation with economic, social, and political matters. He finds nowhere in black religion sustained attention given to matters of theology pertaining to doctrine and liturgy.[45] Black religion is

---

45. Joseph R. Washington Jr., *Black Religion: The Negro and Christianity in the United States* (Boston: Beacon Press, 1964), 139, 143.

thus an instrument or tool for social protest as opposed to an authentic historical expression of Christianity. Washington's claims were convincing to people who saw no African American professional theologians. In academic settings, even in predominantly black schools, no African American theologians focused solely on research, reflection, and writing on issues and concerns in black churches.[46]

Washington's book represented a challenge to black clergy. The challenge, which the National Conference of Black Churchmen took up, was to put black theology into print. The NCBC established a Theological Commission, bringing together black clergy and black scholars in religion and theology in order to make explicit the theology in the black church.[47] The commission was made up mostly of black clergy with a few black seminary professors invited to participate. The aim of the commission was to correct the misconceptions that Washington's book spread.

Prior to the decline of the NCBC, Charles Rooks, then director of the Fund for Theological Education, received a request from the Association of Theological School's Special Commission on the Black Religious Experience to gather African American seminary professors and discuss with them what they might do together in theological education.[48] The result of this gathering and discussion was the formation of the Society for the Study of Black Religion (SSBR). Seminary professors had in effect created an arena of discussion and collaboration on black theology outside of the NCBC. With the SSBR in place, the decline of the NCBC did not disrupt the black theological movement.

Though black religion scholars and academic black theologians have, since the mid-1970s, turned to African American churches as their principal audience, the existence of professional academic forums virtually ensures that academic black theology can be done apart from black church settings. Since the founding of the SSBR, African American seminary professors have formed other professional groups for discussions on black theology. In national and regional meetings of the American Academy of Religion (AAR) and the Society of Biblical Literature (SBL), scholars may explore and further develop black theology as an academic specialty area. The AAR has groups for Black Theology,

---

46. Rooks, *Revolution in Zion*, 121.
47. Cone, *For My People*, 21–24.
48. Rooks, *Revolution in Zion*, 134–35.

Womanist Approaches to Religion and Society, and Afro-American Religious History. The SBL has the African American Theology and Biblical Hermeneutics Group. All these groups convene at the annual meetings of the AAR and SBL. Regional associations of both scholarly societies have similar groups that meet in their yearly gatherings. Quite to the opposite of James Cone's insistence that constructive black liberation theologies are not academic, he concedes that the prevailing trend defines, discusses, and presents black theology primarily within the SSBR, AAR, and SBL.[49]

In addition to the SSBR, AAR, and SBL, academic black theologians participate in forums sponsored by the Black Theology Project (BTP) and the Ecumenical Association of Third World Theologians (EATWOT). The BTP is an ecumenical association of African American Christians formed in 1976 as a result of a 1975 Detroit conference sponsored by the Theology in the Americas, an interracial and predominantly Roman Catholic organization.[50] Theologians from Africa, Asia, and North and Latin America founded EATWOT in 1976. The BTP collaborates with the EATWOT in activities such as conferences, publications, and exchange programs. Though not strictly academic associations, the BTP and EATWOT provide an arena for the development of black theology outside of predominately African American Christian denominations, just as the SSBR, AAR, and SBL do.

As a distinct academic subject or specialty area, black theology is characterized by its own basic problematic. The basic underlying question of academic black theology, approached from various ways, is "What does it mean to be black, Christian, and free?"[51] That is to say, constructive black theology attempts to define, clarify, and reconcile blackness, Christianity, and liberation. The earliest debates and issues revolving around this basic problematic were on the appropriate form that liberation must take (integration or separation?), the use of violence in order to achieve liberation, the desirability and place of racial reconciliation in black liberation, the relation of black religion (and black sources) to black theology as the latter's proper subject

49. Cone, General Introduction to *Black Theology: A Documentary History, Volume Two: 1980–1992*, ed. Cone and Wilmore, 6.

50. Cone, *For My People*, 164; Wilmore, General Introduction to *Black Theology: A Documentary History, 1966–1979*, ed. Cone and Wilmore, 9.

51. Cone, General Introduction to *Black Theology: A Documentary History, Volume Two: 1980–1992*, ed. Cone and Wilmore, 1–2.

matter, and the adequacy of traditional Western theism in black liberation thought.[52] Recent conversations seeking to expand the notion of
liberation to redress classism, sexism, homophobia, ecological devastation, and inaction on the part of the church and clergy in liberation
movements have since augmented the early debates.[53]

As academic black theology has wrestled with its basic problematic
of defining and reconciling blackness, Christianity, and liberation, the
discipline has undergone a unique development and relationship with
respect to both African American churches and institutions of higher
learning. After seminary professors perceived the need to base their
constructive black theologies in African American churches, the entrance of academic black theology into these churches has not been
altogether easy or uncomplicated. This situation of complexity may
be due to what J. Deotis Roberts and Gayraud Wilmore acknowledge
as the existence of two black theologies existing in isolation from each
other.[54] One theology is informal and the other is formal, systematic,
and academic.

By "informal" black theology, Roberts and Wilmore are referring
to the construction of black theology in African American church
and community settings that relies almost exclusively on oral traditions. Outside of academic settings, black intellectuals use preaching
and music as their chief modes for expressing their thoughts.[55] Black
preaching and musical traditions are deeply rooted in black cultural life
and have "accepted rules of procedure, criteria of judgment, canons
for assessing performance, models of past achievement and present
emulation, and an acknowledged succession of superb accomplish-
ments."[56] Albert Raboteau agrees. He says that the traditional art of
black preaching "is governed by strict rules that require skill and dedication to master."[57] According to Raboteau, the black folk sermon

---

52. These debates are the early ones, as identified by James Cone. See his "An Interpretation
of the Debate," Epilogue to *Black Theology: A Documentary History, 1966–1979,* ed. Cone and
Wilmore, 612.

53. Cone, General Introduction to *Black Theology: A Documentary History, Volume Two: 1980–
1992,* ed. Cone and Wilmore, 2–3.

54. J. Deotis Roberts, *The Prophethood of Black Believers: An African American Political Theology
for Ministry* (Louisville, Ky.: Westminster/John Knox Press, 1994), 13.

55. Cornel West, *Keeping Faith: Philosophy and Race in America* (New York: Routledge, 1994),
72–73.

56. Ibid., 73.

57. Albert J. Raboteau, *A Fire in the Bones: Reflections on African-American Religious History*
(Boston: Beacon Press, 1995), 141.

consists of two tracks that run simultaneously during oral performance: one is devoted to content, the information that the speaker
wishes to communicate, and the other is devoted to stylistic performance, the techniques of how the message is spoken.[58] From the sermon,
and even singing, African Americans have come to expect a message
with substantial content (i.e., one that is informational, inspirational,
logically consistent, cogent in argument, etc.) and superb performance
that are together measured by the response evoked from the audience.

According to two pollings conducted by *Ebony* magazine, the most
popular and widely circulated African American publication, the most
outstanding African American preachers in the 1993 ranking are Gard-
ner C. Taylor, Jeremiah A. Wright Jr., Samuel D. Proctor, Charles G.
Adams, Otis Moss Jr., H. Beecher Hicks Jr., Jesse L. Jackson Sr.,
James A. Forbes Jr., Caesar A. W. Clark, Wyatt T. Walker, Joseph E.
Lowery, John Hurst Adams, Manuel L. Scott Sr., Frederick G. Samp-
son, and J. Alfred Smith Sr.; the 1997 ranking of women preachers
cited Prathia Hall, Vashti M. McKenzie, Carolyn Ann Knight, Renita J.
Weems, Suzan Johnson-Cook, Ann Farrar Lightner-Fuller, Delores H.
Carpenter, Claudette A. Copeland, Jacqueline E. McCullough, Ernes-
tine Cleveland Reems, Yvonne Delk, Johnnie Colemon, Ella Pearson
Mitchell, Barbara L. King, and Jessica Kendall Ingram.[59] While most
of these preachers in the national ranking have seminary and graduate theological education, and even hold doctorate degrees in various
disciplines, none of them are full-time professional systematic theologians. None of the leading academic black theologians who I examine
in chapters 2, 3, and 4 were recognized in this ranking, except for
Jacquelyn Grant, who received honorable mention in the 1997 poll. If
the question is raised, "To whom are African Americans listening?" or
"To whom do African Americans turn for wisdom and inspiration?"
the answer would be, "They are turning to intellectuals in the black
oral tradition."

By "formal" black theology, Roberts and Wilmore refer to the con-

58. Ibid., 142–44.
59. "The 15 Greatest Black Preachers," *Ebony* 49, no. 1 (November 1993): 156–58, 160,
162, 164, 166, 168; "The 15 Greatest Black Women Preachers," *Ebony* 53, no. 1 (November
1997): 102–4, 106, 108, 110, 112, 114. The *Ebony* polls are not conducted regularly. For past
assessments of popularity of African American clergy, see "America's 15 Greatest Black Preachers," *Ebony* 39, no. 1 (November 1984): 27–30, and "Great Negro Preachers: Ten Most Popular
Ministers Lead Vigorous Public Lives," *Ebony* 9, no. 9 (July 1954): 26–30.

struction of black theology in academic settings, that is, in scholarly societies, seminaries, divinity schools, and departments of religion that results in the creation of written works. According to Lincoln and Mamiya, the radical reformist and revolutionary construal of liberation by academic black theology is at odds with the more prevalent construals of liberation by African American church intellectuals in the ideologies of economic uplift and self-help.[60] Dialogue and collaboration between academic black theologians and black church intellectuals has been rare. Reflecting on his participation in a recent workshop with black theologians and black church leaders sponsored by the Kelly Miller Smith Institute on African American Church Studies, James Cone says that their attempts at dialogue, as he had observed before between academic black theologians and black church intellectuals, was marked by suspicion and mistrust.[61]

The suspicion of church leaders may be due, in part, to the narrow focus of academic black theologians. Black church intellectuals have little or no role in the selection and determination of canons or standards that academic black theologians use. African American churches, as a whole, do not control or set the standards of those educational institutions wherein academic black theologians pursue their research and teaching. Furthermore, the radical tendency that academic black theologians emphasize usually overshadows and, at worst, excludes those tendencies and aspects of African American religion of concern to black church leaders.

For black church leaders like the late Joseph H. Jackson, the notion of liberation is not contemptible. Jackson's objection to the new black theology was not against the theme of liberation. He was incensed with academic black theologians' neglect of other important aspects of black churches like evangelism, reaching out to all people, and spiritual transformations resulting in personal as well as social improvements.[62] Church leaders, who must attend to various dimensions of their respective faith communities, find distasteful, for example, Gayraud Wilmore's claim that black radicalism "has been the most

---

60. Lincoln and Mamiya, *The Black Church in the African American Experience,* 182–83.

61. Cone, General Introduction to *Black Theology: A Documentary History, Volume Two: 1980–1992,* ed. Cone and Wilmore, 6.

62. Joseph H. Jackson, "The Basic Theological Position of the National Baptist Convention, U.S.A., Inc." (September 1971), in *Black Theology: A Documentary History, 1966–1980,* ed. Cone and Wilmore, 260–61.

distinctive, persistent, and valuable part of the religious heritage of African Americans in the United States." Another point of contention is black theology's political intention to be the principal, perhaps only, voice of and for oppressed African Americans. Consider what Kelly Brown Douglas says about the political intentions of academic black theology.

Douglas claims that womanist theology does not emerge from institutions of higher learning. Instead, "it emerges from the life, wisdom, and faith of black women struggling for the well-being of their families and themselves."[63] In what seems to be a contradiction, Douglas contends that womanist theology, which is taught in institutions of higher learning, must be propagated in African American churches and communities.[64] She is correct to emphasize the relevance of academic womanist theology to what is happening in these churches and communities. However, she fails to make the case for the special authority of academic womanist theology. She assumes that the return, or better still the turn, of academic womanist theology to African American churches and communities has something more to say than that which is already spoken in these churches and communities.

Wilmore echoes Douglas's notion of the academic theologian's returning to the community. Wilmore claims that "the purpose of graduate theological education...[is] to prepare men and women to convey the results of their academic research and reflection to people who have no degrees, and in many cases not even a decent secondary education."[65] Though probably well intended, academic black theologians' sharing of information is usually met with suspicion and distrust. Persons in African American communities who lack formal education and academic degrees perceive the gestures of black academics as condescending behavior, which perhaps are not altogether unfounded perceptions. Lack of academic degrees and formal education does not mean that a person is incapable of serious thought and critical reflection. Moreover, as I just mentioned, the black oral tradition contains rules, criteria, models, and so forth that dis-

---

63. Kelly Brown Douglas, "Teaching Womanist Theology," in *Living the Intersection: Womanism and Afrocentrism in Theology*, ed. Cheryl J. Sanders (Minneapolis: Fortress Press, 1995), 154.

64. Ibid., 155.

65. Gayraud S. Wilmore, Preface to *African American Religious Studies: An Interdisciplinary Anthology*, ed. Gayraud S. Wilmore (Durham, N.C.: Duke University Press, 1989), vii.

cipline thought. The oral tradition is capable of producing its own intellectuals.

The distinction between formal and informal black theology and the rivalry between professional theologians and church leaders obfuscates the relation of black theology's articulation in academic settings to its oral transmission in church and community settings. Several black theologians are themselves members of African American churches and very much involved in the affairs of their communities. Their theological reflection is not divorced totally from oral traditions. These professional theologians represent faithfully the oral traditions to which they have been exposed.

## WOMANIST THOUGHT, BLACK CATHOLIC THEOLOGY, AND GLOBALIZATION

Since the mid-1970s, academic black theology has hardly been a discussion between black male Protestant thinkers only. Criticism (external and internal), demands for inclusion (by women and other suppressed groups within African American communities), discovery of new or previously neglected sources, and a bit of daring on the part of black theologians to explore new directions in thought have broadened academic black theology's range of concerns. Promising developments include womanist theology, black Catholic theology, and cross-cultural dialogue with Third World theologians.

The black theological movement's earliest stages of development focused mostly on the task of legitimization.[66] In seeking to establish black theology as an authentic Christian theology, black theologians attacked prevalent theologies and mainline Christian denominations as expressions of "white theology" and therefore racist and oblivious to the experience and contributions of African Americans to Christian thought. White theologians ignored and, in rare instances, condemned this nascent black theology. However, black theology evoked sympathetic and critical response from several white theologians — for example, in Europe, George Casalis, Bruno Chenu, Helmut Gollwitzer,

---

66. William R. Jones, "Toward an Interim Assessment of Black Theology," *Christian Century* 89 (May 3, 1972): 515.

Jürgen Moltmann, Henry Mottu, and Theo Witvliet; and in North America, Glenn R. Bucher, John Carey, G. Clarke Chapman Jr., Frederick Herzog, Peter C. Hodgson, Paul Lehman, Benjamin Reist, and Rosemary Radford Ruether.[67]

Ruether's assessment of black theology anticipates the development of womanist theology.[68] As early as 1974, Ruether identified the limitations of both black theology (mostly done by black males) and feminist theology (mostly done by white females) as frameworks of interpretation for African American women. According to Ruether, interconnecting oppression by sex, race, and class creates tensions between white women and black women, between black men and white women, and between black men and black women.[69] The solution that she sees is and must be an autonomous theological enterprise conducted by black women. Earliest work and publications in this independent black womanist thought include those of Theressa Hoover, Pauli Murray, Letty Russell, Katie Cannon, and Jacquelyn Grant. The field today includes many other scholars, such as Karen Baker-Fletcher, M. Shawn Copeland, Jualynne Dodson, Kelly Brown Douglas, Toinette Eugene, Cheryl Townsend Gilkes, Diana Hayes, Renee Hill, Cheryl Kirk-Duggan, Clarice Martin, Jamie Phelps, Marcia Riggs, Cheryl Sanders, Linda E. Thomas, Emilie Townes, Alice Walker, Renita Weems, and Delores Williams, each exploring various aspects of black women's experience from her disciplinary perspective with the ultimate intention of developing a holistic theology that comprehends not only issues pertaining to gender but also sexuality, race, class, and ecology. The entry of more capable African American women in the fields of theological and religious studies continues to enlarge womanist thought.

Besides African American women, black Catholics are a suppressed voice in black theology. As of 1998, about 2.3 million African Amer-

---

67. Gayraud S. Wilmore, Foreword to Theo Witvliet's *The Way of the Black Messiah: The Hermeneutical Challenge of Black Theology as a Theology of Liberation* (Oak Park, Ill.: Meyer-Stone, 1987), vi–vii; James H. Cone, Introduction to Part III: Black Theology and the Response of White Theologians, *Black Theology: A Documentary History, 1966–1979,* ed. Cone and Wilmore, 138, 139.

68. Rosemary Radford Ruether, "Crisis in Sex and Race: Black Theology vs. Feminist Theology," *Christianity and Crisis* 34 (April 15, 1974): 67–73.

69. Rosemary Radford Ruether, *New Woman/New Earth: Sexist Ideologies and Human Liberation* (New York: Seabury Press, 1975), 166.

ican Catholics lived in the United States.[70] Lincoln and Mamiya estimate that 86 percent of African American Christians have membership in black-controlled organizations.[71] They limit their study of the black church to "independent, historic, and totally black controlled denominations," namely, the African Methodist Episcopal Church; African Methodist Episcopal Church Zion; Christian Methodist Episcopal Church; Church of God in Christ; National Baptist Convention, U.S.A.; National Baptist Convention of America; and Progressive National Baptist Convention. About 80 percent of African American Christians have membership in these seven denominations. Indeed, the predominant religious tradition among African Americans is evangelical Protestant Christianity.

The covering term "black church," however, must consciously include African American Catholics who do have significant presence, involvement, and historical roots in African American communities. Concerns and emphases in black Catholic theology are with oppression (both within society and the church), the role and presence of Mary and other doctrines unique to the Roman Catholic Church, the universal aspect of the church (the meaning of catholic), human diversity and interrelationship (social, cultural, and religious pluralism), and church theology (liturgy, worship, spirituality, etc., that appreciates African heritage and African American culture). Persons contributing to the field of black Catholic theology include: Edward Braxton, M. Shawn Copeland, Toinette Eugene, Diana Hayes, Philip Linden, Bryan Massingale, Jamie Phelps, and Thaddeus Posey. Shawn Copeland has served as director of the Black Theology Project and written summaries of the black theological movement among Catholics.[72]

Identification of liberation as the content, the essential theme, of Christianity has led to dialogue between and comparative studies of black theology and other forms of liberation theology. The term "globalization" should not be taken to mean that black theology is embraced worldwide. Instead, globalization should be understood as

---

70. Cyprian Davis and Diana L. Hayes, eds., *Taking Down Our Harps: Black Catholics in the United States* (Maryknoll, N.Y.: Orbis Books, 1998), xv.

71. Lincoln and Mamiya, *The Black Church,* 1, 411 n. 3.

72. M. Shawn Copeland, "Method in Emerging Black Catholic Theology," 120–44, in *Taking Down Our Harps;* idem, "African American Catholics and Black Theology: An Interpretation," 99–115, in *Black Theology: A Documentary History, Volume Two: 1980–1992.*

cross-cultural dialogue between African American men and women themselves and their engagement with intellectual traditions and African, Asian, and Latin American theologians, and even European and North American theologians interested in the interpretation and relevance of Christianity for social transformation. Though too numerous to list here, some of these dialogical and comparative studies include: Frederick Herzog's *Liberation Theology* (1972); Peter C. Hodgson's *Children of Freedom* (1974) and *New Birth of Freedom* (1976); Benjamin Reist's *Theology in Red, White, and Black* (1975); Cornel West's *Prophesy Deliverance* (1982); J. Deotis Roberts's *Black Theology in Dialogue* (1987); Theo Witvliet's *The Way of the Black Messiah* (1987); Dwight Hopkins's *Black Theology U.S.A. and South Africa* (1989); Josiah U. Young's *Black and African Theologies* (1986) and *A Pan-African Theology* (1992); George C. L. Cummings's *A Common Journey* (1993); and Garth and Karen Baker-Fletcher's *My Sister, My Brother* (1997).

## SUMMARY

This chapter relates academic black theology to African American religious life; competing informal, unsystematic but more prevalent formulations of black theology in African American churches and communities; and the political intentions and personal aspirations of scholars in the field of academic black theology. Black theology was not new or unique in the 1960s. In African American life, a longstanding tendency has been to relate religion, positively or negatively, to the experience of blackness. Neither liberation nor any other theme is essential to the definition of black theology. When negative aspects of blackness — that is, sufferings from economic, social, and political oppression — are the matter of greatest concern, black theology takes on a liberation orientation. When survival, cultural fulfillment, and knowledge are matters of concern, empowerment and self-understanding become prominent themes in black theology. Academic black theology's hermeneutical turn to black sources in the construction of liberation theologies is evidence of the existence of black theology prior to the 1960s.

Lincoln and Mamiya's recent sociological survey documenting alternative liberation traditions suggests that academic black constructive theologies are not the only possible formulations of black theology. The political intention and personal ambition of academic black theologians to be the voice of and for oppressed African Americans further expose the limitations of academic black theology. Their intentions and ambitions reflect their adoption of a competitive and sometimes condescending posture toward other black intellectuals. Academic black theology is in a position of competition among oral traditions of black theology in African American churches and communities; academic black theology is also in a position of tension posed by internal competition among the distinct methodological perspectives used by theologians in this field.

This chapter's demonstration of the relativity of academic black theology does not by itself displace academic black theology. The unsettling of academic black theology is not a simple task. Academic black theology has made African American theological studies a real possibility in institutions of higher learning. Prior to the contemporary black theological movement in seminaries and divinity schools, African Americans could not study and concentrate on African American religion as a legitimate academic subject area. The academic turn of black theology made the study and interpretation of African American religious thought a genuine possibility in institutions of higher learning. However, the unfortunate consequence of academic black theology's presence in institutions of higher learning is the lack of awareness of the multiple ways in which it can be, and is, done outside the halls of academia. Chapters 2, 3, and 4 analyze academic black theology in its three schools of thought, each of which represents a unique way of doing black theology.

# CHAPTER TWO

# The Black Hermeneutical School

**C**HARLES B. COPHER, a biblical scholar at the Interdenominational Theological Center, raised the earliest awareness of a shared methodological perspective among black theologians. In the Black Biblical Consultation held during the annual meeting of the Society of Biblical Literature in 1984, Copher read from a paper discussing the differences between James H. Cone, Henry H. Mitchell, Joseph A. Johnson, Major J. Jones, Robert A. Bennett, and William Mason relative to their shared quest for a "black hermeneutic."[1] That paper was published recently in an anthology of Copher's works in 1993.[2]

In Copher's attempt to understand the meaning of the term "black hermeneutic" for these black theologians, he concluded that the term is most certainly not synonymous with "exegesis," though these theologians are interested in and engage in critical interpretation of the Bible. The term refers to the retrieval of the message of the "Black Fathers," that is, black pastors serving churches under black control from the late eighteenth century to the early twentieth century. "Black hermeneutic" also refers to use of methods of interpretation that ensure consistency with the theme of liberation in that message.[3]

Because Copher's study discloses the quest for a black hermeneutic as a definitive quality in this earliest detected shared perspective, I call this perspective the Black Hermeneutical School. In James Cone's rec-

---

1. Gayraud S. Wilmore, Introduction to Part III: New Directions in Black Biblical Interpretation, *Black Theology: A Documentary History, Volume Two: 1980–1992*, ed. Cone and Wilmore, 178–79. Wilmore says that Copher read an earlier version of this paper at a conference held in the year 1970. See Charles B. Copher, *Black Biblical Studies: An Anthology of Charles B. Copher: Biblical and Theological Issues on the Black Presence in the Bible* (Chicago: Black Light Fellowship, 1993), 3.
2. Copher, "African Americans and Biblical Hermeneutics: Black Interpretation of the Bible," chap. 5, *Black Biblical Studies*, 67–77.
3. Ibid., 69–71, 75.

ollections on his involvement in the black theological movement, in *My Soul Looks Back* (1986), he says, "My severe criticism of the black church in *Black Theology and Black Power* (1969) arose out of my conviction that it had failed to remain faithful to its heritage of freedom."[4] This self-criticism which he sought to bring to the black churches is an attempt to recapture the faith and religiosity that he believes is unique to African American religious communities.[5]

## THINKERS

The largest and most diversified of the three schools of academic black theology is the Black Hermeneutical School. This school includes such thinkers as Katie G. Cannon, Albert B. Cleage, Cecil Cone, James H. Cone, Kelly Brown Douglas, James H. Evans, Jacquelyn Grant, Dwight N. Hopkins, Major J. Jones, Olin P. Moyd, J. Deotis Roberts, Delores S. Williams, and Gayraud S. Wilmore. Cleage, who changed his name to Jarumogi Abebe Agyman in 1970, published *The Black Messiah* (1968), a collection of sermons grounded in the affirmation of the blackness of Christ and the construal of Christianity as a form of black nationalism. Though not technically a work in systematic theology, Cleage's book was the first text in the black theological movement. Cecil Cone and Gayraud Wilmore have argued for the recognition of black religion as the principal source and subject matter of black theology. James Cone has exerted the greatest influence in this school of thought. He published the first two systematic theological works in contemporary black theology, *Black Theology and Black Power* (1969) and *A Black Theology of Liberation* (1970). He has since remained the most prolific writer in academic black theology. Also, more than any other black theologian, he has committed himself to the doctoral education of African Americans in theology. Wilmore has gone so far as to say that "Cone's most enduring contribution is the training of younger Black scholars who have taken doctoral degrees under him at Union."[6]

Katie Cannon, Mark L. Chapman, George C. L. Cummings, Kelly

---

4. Cone, *My Soul Looks Back,* 79.
5. Ibid., 70.
6. Gayraud S. Wilmore, Introduction to Part III: Theological and Ethical Studies, *African American Religious Studies,* ed. Gayraud S. Wilmore, 173.

Brown Douglas, James Evans, Cain H. Felder, Jacquelyn Grant, Dwight Hopkins, Alonzo Johnson, Sandy D. Martin, Preston R. Washington, Dennis W. Wiley, Delores Williams, and Josiah U. Young were once students at Union Theological Seminary/Columbia University, where Cone has taught since 1969. However, they have not replicated Cone's work. They have made original contributions to academic black theology. For example, Evans's and Hopkins's works concentrated on the development of black theology as a systematic theology. Evans's *We Have Been Believers* (1992) is the first comprehensive systematic construction of black theology since James Cone's publication of *God of the Oppressed* in 1975. Hopkins's work covers the identification, evaluation, and use of primary sources for black theological construction. Cannon, Grant, and Williams have constructed feminist critiques of the black theological movement, pointing out the oversight of African American women's experience in black theological discourse. The influence of Union's program in black theology and its graduates' teaching, advocacy, and publications (a large number through Orbis Books) is so great that a majority of readers of black theology mistakenly assume that black theology is one and the same with Union Seminary and Orbis Books.

James Cone credits Gayraud Wilmore with the theological expertise and imagination that laid the foundation for the early development of contemporary black theology.[7] He says, "More than any other organization, the [National Conference of Black Churchmen] was responsible for providing the context for the development of black theology."[8] Wilmore served as the first chairman of the NCBC's theological commission and was chief writer of most of its public statements.

Gayraud Wilmore contends that J. Deotis Roberts has developed the most significant contrasting perspective to that of James Cone.[9] Olin Moyd wrote his dissertation project, later published as *Redemption in Black Theology* (1979), under Roberts's supervision. Roberts was a member of the NCBC's theological commission, as was Cone. I think that Wilmore's claim is that Cone, a systematic theologian, and

7. Cone, *For My People*, 18.
8. Ibid.
9. Wilmore, Introduction to Part III: Theological and Ethical Studies, *African American Religious Studies*, 174.

Roberts, a philosophical theologian, more than any other thinkers in the Black Hermeneutical School, deal comprehensively with a wide spectrum of issues in black theology. So, significant differences exist between Roberts and Cone, between male and female theologians, and between any other thinkers named above. Yet, as I shall attempt to show, each operates within a shared methodological perspective.

## TASKS

In the Black Hermeneutical School, the tasks of black theology — with varying degrees of emphasis — are description, analysis, evaluation, explanation, and revision. Commenting on the descriptive and explanatory tasks of black theology, James Cone says:

> Our task is not to tell others what the gospel is, as if we know and they do not. Our task rather is to take as the content for black theology the pre-reflective understanding of the gospel had by black Christians, in order to make their voices heard throughout the churches and society. We do not create the gospel; we interpret it as it is celebrated in worship and as it is practiced in society. Deeply embedded in black church history are the sermons, songs, and prayers of our grandparents waiting to be put into a theological language that can serve as a guide for our contemporary efforts to be faithful.[10]

To what Cone says, Major Jones adds:

> The Black theologian's task must encompass the responsibility of deriving a systematic, critical evaluation and rational defense of what has been interpreted as the central meaning of the Christian faith. This central meaning must then translate into both personal and collective commitments and subsequent meaningful actions.[11]

The task of revision is construed primarily as a correction of the omissions made by "white theology" and reconceptualization of cardinal beliefs in Christianity, such as beliefs about God, humanity, Christ,

---

10. Cone, *For My People*, 117.
11. Major J. Jones, *The Color of God: The Concept of God in Afro-American Thought* (Macon, Ga.: Mercer University Press, 1987), 2.

church, and eschatology.[12] Revision is not emphasized now as much as when contemporary academic black theology began. According to James Cone, in order to dislodge Christianity from its negative portrayal as a "white religion," black theologians sought to uncover the demonic and sinister nature of white religion as something apart from Christianity.[13] This zeal for revision led to academic black theology's fixation on white racism in white churches and American society.[14] Black theologians found themselves in the predicament of reacting more negatively toward white racism than positively toward the history and culture of African Americans.[15]

At the insistence of Gayraud Wilmore, Charles Long, Henry Mitchell, and Cecil Cone, black religion came to be identified as the proper foundation and subject matter of black theology by black theologians.[16] In abandoning a mere reactionary mode of scholarship, these thinkers looked to black religion in search of African Americans' unique responses to divine reality. For example, James Cone's *The Spirituals and the Blues* (1972); *Cut Loose Your Stammering Tongue* (1991), edited by George Cummings and Dwight Hopkins; Riggins R. Earl's *Dark Symbols, Obscure Signs* (1993); Hopkins's *Shoes That Fit Our Feet* (1993) and *Down, Up, and Over* (2000); David E. Goatley's *Were You There?* (1996); Cheryl A. Kirk-Duggan's *Exorcizing Evil* (1997); Donald H. Matthews's *Honoring the Ancestors* (1998); and Will E. Coleman's *Tribal Talk* (2000) are representative of the increasing studies of songs, narratives, folklore, and other black cultural sources that convey religious meanings in African American life.

The descriptive, analytical, explanatory, and evaluative tasks of theology are evident in the concern of black theologians to describe or state accurately the religious faith of African Americans and to point out the moral imperatives that faith implies. James Cone asserts that the truth of Christian faith is already given.[17] The task of the black theologian then becomes the act of making explicit that which is implied in African Americans' understanding of Christian faith as they

---

12. Roberts, *Black Theology Today*, 58, 60.
13. Cone, *For My People*, 40.
14. Ibid., 86.
15. Ibid., 87.
16. Cone, "An Interpretation of the Debate among Black Theologians," Epilogue to *Black Theology: A Documentary History, 1966–1979*, ed. Cone and Wilmore, 616–17.
17. Cone, *A Black Theology of Liberation*, Twentieth Anniversary Edition, 8.

celebrate it in worship and practice. James Evans agrees with Cone that the primary task of black theology is to assess the truth that is already given in the community of faith.[18]

James Evans prefers to call the task of revision "deconstruction." He acknowledges the fact that deconstructionism is a movement associated with modern French intellectuals. In his opinion, deconstruction is both iconoclastic and constructive, dismantling intellectual systems for the purpose of exposing new possibilities for thought. He says, "Nascent black theology embodied this dual character [of deconstructionism] to the extent that it employed a hermeneutics of suspicion and a hermeneutics of restoration. In short, it was both a project of iconoclasm and a project of retrieval."[19] Black theology revisions Christian faith and theology by scrutinizing European American theology and utilizing the experiences of African Americans as a point of departure for theological construction.

Evans goes on to summarize the tasks of black theology in what he sees as three endeavors that the black theologian must undertake.[20] The first endeavor is to clarify the contexts (historical, sociopolitical, cultural, and intellectual) wherein African American religious faith is affirmed. In other words, the theologian must make African American religious faith understandable, probe its depth and make clear its meanings with respect to the historical, sociopolitical, cultural, and intellectual situations under which African Americans have lived. Evans has in mind life under slavery, the struggle for civil rights, and resistance to and revision of ideas and values linked to racial oppression. The second endeavor is to articulate, interpret, and assess the essential doctrinal affirmations of African American faith for the contemporary African American community of faith. Through this endeavor he wants the black theologian to "tell a story that relates the hope of the biblical message with the [often harsh realities] of black experience."[21] The third endeavor is to examine the moral implications of African American faith for Christian witness in the world. In other words, black theologians must suggest how to live out Christian faith. The

---

18. James H. Evans Jr., *We Have Been Believers: An African American Systematic Theology* (Minneapolis: Fortress Press, 1992), 31.

19. Evans, "Deconstructing the Tradition," 103.

20. Evans, *We Have Been Believers,* 3–9.

21. Ibid., 32.

theologian must develop norms for judgment and action. Evans contends that this third task is the goal of black theology: action that leads to the liberation of oppressed peoples.

Delores Williams and Katie Cannon discuss the tasks of black theology primarily from the point of view of the womanist theologian and ethicist. Williams contends that three intentions (dialogical, liturgical, and didactic) and one basic commitment should determine the activity of the theologian.[22] These three intentional acts are: (1) to advocate and participate in dialogue and action with many diverse social, political, and religious communities concerned about human survival, liberation, and fulfillment; (2) to reflect in one's theology but also critique the thought, worship, and action of African American churches; and (3) to teach Christians new insights about a moral life based on ethics that supports justice for women and survival, liberation, and fulfillment for all humans. The fundamental commitment of the womanist theologian is to use rational argument; valid methods of research; and women's history, culture, religious experience, and female imagery and metaphor in theological construction.

For Cannon, the womanist theologian and ethicist should engage in four areas of activity: (1) pedagogy (teaching), (2) methodology (mapping the logic, procedures, and perimeters of one's field of study), (3) revision (critique of male bias and substantial omissions of women's experience in theology, ethics, and religious history), and (4) construction (articulating the existential realities and wisdom of African American women).[23] Yet, according to Cannon, the womanist's principal task, which determines and becomes the measure of all of her other tasks, is to speak simultaneously to the universality of the human condition and to the particularities of race, sex, and class oppression in black women's experience.

## CONTENT

For the Black Hermeneutical School, liberation is the content of black theology. This theme of liberation is understood primarily within the

---

22. Delores S. Williams, "Womanist Theology: Black Women's Voices," in *Black Theology: A Documentary History, Volume Two: 1980–1992,* ed. Cone and Wilmore, 269–71.

23. Katie G. Cannon, *Katie's Canon: Womanism and the Soul of the Black Community* (New York: Continuum, 1995), 69–70.

context of biblical tradition. In James Cone's *A Black Theology of Liberation* (1970), he declares that liberation is the principal theme of black theology.[24] For him, the meaning of liberation is expressed primarily within the context of the Bible. In other words, the Bible provides his model of liberation. For him, the meaning of liberation, which is best illustrated in the exodus of the Hebrews from Egyptian slavery, is told in the Old Testament. Cone asserts that the physical release of the Hebrews from slavery is analogous to what African Americans are seeking — a political transformation in this life. In the New Testament, he asserts that Jesus' identification and ministry among the poor and his labor to bring all humanity into the kingdom of God indicates God's intention to liberate humanity from "all powers that threaten human life."[25]

In addition to defining the theme of liberation using biblical texts in witness to God's liberating activity, black folk stories also exemplify a determination for freedom.[26] James Evans asserts that in slave testimony, folklore, personal narratives, and so forth, African Americans describe what freedom means to them and express their hopes of attaining it. James Cone agrees with Evans but insists that the Bible be held in dialectical tension with not only black folk stories but with the stories of other oppressed peoples.[27] For Cone, "the Bible is a liberating word for many people but not the *only* word of liberation."[28]

In challenge to James Cone's earliest systematic work in *A Black Theology of Liberation,* other black theologians such as J. Deotis Roberts, Major Jones, Olin Moyd, and Delores Williams have sought to clarify further the theme of liberation and demonstrate its relation to other themes such as reconciliation, hope, redemption, and survival. Roberts contends that liberation must be understood within the context of reconciliation. From his point of view, "Christianity is rooted in the belief that God was in Christ reconciling the world to Godself (2 Cor. 5:19), and that reconciliation between God and humans can be effected only

---

24. Cone, *A Black Theology of Liberation,* Twentieth Anniversary Edition, 4.
25. Ibid., 3.
26. Evans, *We Have Been Believers,* 6–7, 24–26.
27. James H. Cone, *God of the Oppressed,* Revised with new introduction (San Francisco: Harper & Row, Seabury Press, 1975; Maryknoll, N.Y.: Orbis Books, 1997), xi.
28. Ibid.

through reconciliation between persons."[29] Within this context of reconciliation, liberation for Roberts means the freedom of the oppressed to enter into new relations with their former oppressors.

Major Jones agrees with J. Deotis Roberts's definition of liberation within the context of reconciliation, but Jones emphasizes the necessity of presenting a clear vision of the nature or features of this reconciliation. He therefore emphasizes the theme of hope — eschatological expectation — in black liberation theology. He contends that black theology must present a clear vision of the future where the oppressed and oppressors are redeemed and reconciled in a community not of their own making but of God's. In Jones's view, in this community where black identity "will be no problem, for identity will have been achieved and within a climate wherein it will be fully recognized, fully accepted, and fully respected. There will be pluralism of ideologies, interests, aims and aspirations, and personhood; and no one will for any purpose be denied opportunity to achieve, or be excluded from community."[30]

Olin Moyd contends that redemption, which encompasses both liberation and confederation, is the central theme in black religious thought.[31] He defines redemption as "salvation from sin and guilt and salvation from oppression."[32] According to Moyd, the concern of African Americans has been with both overcoming sin — that is, personal moral failure — and overcoming economic, social, and political oppression. He defines liberation as radical freedom, that is, "a state of salvation from human-caused and human-imposed disabilities and constraints all over this world."[33] Moyd defines confederation as "the forming of a community, local and universal, of the chosen people of God resulting from their understanding of the will of God, also the practice of a life-style which is consistent with the fulfillment of a covenant relationship with God."[34] In Moyd's opinion, the black church is a confederation of redeemed people.[35] Through spiritual care, worship,

---

29. J. Deotis Roberts, *Liberation and Reconciliation: A Black Theology,* Revised edition (Philadelphia: Westminster Press, 1971; reprinted, Maryknoll, N.Y.: Orbis Books, 1994), 9.
30. Jones, *Black Awareness,* 142–43.
31. Olin P. Moyd, *Redemption in Black Theology* (Valley Forge, Pa.: Judson Press, 1979), 8.
32. Ibid., 24.
33. Ibid.
34. Ibid., 23–24.
35. Ibid., 193.

celebration, fellowship, and so forth, the black church is a source and nurturing place for redemption.

If I understand Moyd correctly, he wants to recommend the term "redemption" as a broader term than "liberation." Most people, among whom he includes himself, understand liberation to mean deliverance from economic, social, and political oppression. As Moyd sees it, within the context of the Bible, redemption is inclusive of deliverance from economic, social, and political oppression as well as deliverance from sin (i.e., personal moral failure and the guilt and self-hatred that accompany it), sickness, trouble, and any other ills that diminish the quality of human life. Moyd correctly points out that the concept of redemption is applicable to God's saving activity in many kinds of situations: in the Old Testament, as the deliverance of the Hebrews from slavery, warring enemies, and exile and as the rescue of individuals from troubles of all sorts; and in the New Testament, as salvation from sin.[36]

Delores Williams posits two African American traditions of biblical hermeneutics for understanding God's activity among the oppressed. She names these traditions "the liberation tradition of African American biblical appropriation" and "the survival/quality-of-life tradition of African American biblical appropriation."[37] She contends that black male theologians have given attention to the former to the virtual exclusion of the latter. According to Williams, African Americans read the Bible with an interest in both liberation and survival. The tradition emphasizing liberation takes as its paradigms the exodus of the Hebrews from Egypt in the Old Testament and Jesus' description of his mission and ministry in terms of liberation in Luke 4 of the New Testament. The survivalist tradition emphasizes how God acts to improve the quality of oppressed people's lives and promote the building of their communities now, before some future event of liberation. The survivalist tradition takes as its paradigm Hagar, the Egyptian slave of Abraham and Sarah. After Hagar and her son Ishmael were put out of Abraham's home and left to fend for themselves in the wilderness, God intervened. God provided them with water, food, and eventually made Ishmael a man of prominence and a patriarch around whom a

---

36. Ibid., 36–54.
37. Delores S. Williams, *Sisters in the Wilderness: The Challenge of Womanist God-Talk* (Maryknoll, N.Y.: Orbis Books, 1993), 2, 5–6.

new community was built. Williams contends that the much needed emphasis of the survivalist/quality-of-life tradition is this: "Liberation is an ultimate [goal], but in the meantime, survival and prosperity must be the experience of [oppressed] people."[38]

James Cone's response to his critics has been to redefine liberation as (1) relationship with God, (2) self-actualization, (3) protest and struggle for freedom, and (4) hope.[39] According to Cone, with respect to relationship with God, liberation means the freedom to relate to God both personally and in communal worship settings. With respect to self-actualization, liberation means the freedom to be the self that God has created one to be. For both the oppressed and oppressors, this freedom is from distorted conceptions of self and hindrances to actualizing each person's potential. Protest and struggle for freedom are indicative of liberation in the form of God's immediate presence among the oppressed in empowering them to resist evil and live.

According to James Cone, most black theologians during the early period of the black theological movement viewed only racism as the problem to be overcome in order to achieve liberation. He asserts that as black theologians have increasingly understood oppression, their understanding of liberation has expanded to now include struggle against and overthrow of sexism, classism, homophobia, and ecological devastation.[40] With respect to hope, liberation refers to oppressed people's apprehension of greater possibilities beyond whatever liberties they have won through protest and struggle. In the form of hope, liberation is manifest in oppressed people's recognition that they need not settle with what they have now; they can and should expect God's best.

Despite the differences between Cone, Roberts, Jones, Moyd, and Williams, they essentially agree on at least three points. First, each considers liberation to be of ultimate importance. The positions of Roberts, Jones, Moyd, and Williams are not rejection of liberation but rather attempts to define what liberation is and how it relates to other themes. Second, each sees liberation as God's act. Humans cannot do liberation alone. Gayraud Wilmore says that in traditional black Christianity, the reign of God does not come by social action programs but

---

38. Ibid., 196.
39. Cone, *God of the Oppressed,* 141–62.
40. Cone, General Introduction to *Black Theology: A Documentary Witness, Volume Two: 1980–1992,* ed. Cone and Wilmore, 2–3.

rather by catastrophe in human history.[41] Third, each sees the future as determined. The future is not open-ended. Liberation is a definite goal or end of human history.

James Evans attempts to summarize the meaning of liberation. He contends that liberation is multidimensional: physical, spiritual, and cultural.[42] By physical, he means that liberation involves freedom of movement, release from physical bondage, and having one's bodily needs and desires fulfilled. By spiritual, he means that liberation involves one's coming into an awareness or understanding of one's worth as a human being in relation to God and others. By cultural, he means that liberation involves freedom from assault by negative self-images, symbols, and stereotypes devised for oppression.

## SOURCES

As black theologians in the Black Hermeneutical School carry out their declared tasks, they make use of several sources. Early into the contemporary black theological movement, James Cone identified six sources of black theology: black experience, black history, black culture, revelation, scripture, and tradition.[43] In an effort to be more precise, Cone narrowed black experience, history, and culture into specific sources such as sermons, prayers, religious and secular songs (e.g., spirituals and the blues), folktales, personal narratives, black literature, worship, and spirituality.[44]

To the already expanding list of indigenous black sources, James Evans adds the African American worldview: black people's understanding of and thought concerning reality as structured by their experiences.[45] Also, to the list of indigenous black sources, Dwight Hopkins adds folklore (especially trickster tales); slave religion; black women's experience and spirituality; and the political theology, ethics, and social vision of black protest leaders.[46] Gayraud Wilmore adds to the list the lower-class black community, that is, the folk religion

---

41. Gayraud S. Wilmore, *Last Things First* (Philadelphia: Westminster Press, 1982), 95.
42. Evans, *We Have Been Believers,* 16–18.
43. Cone, *A Black Theology of Liberation,* Twentieth Anniversary Edition, 23–35.
44. Cone, *God of the Oppressed,* 16–30.
45. Evans, *We Have Been Believers,* 27, 29.
46. Dwight N. Hopkins, *Shoes That Fit Our Feet: Sources for a Constructive Black Theology* (Maryknoll, N.Y.: Orbis Books, 1993), 8–9.

of poor African Americans; the writings, sermons, and addresses of outstanding black preachers and public figures; and African traditional religions.[47] Cecil Cone contends that characteristics of African traditional religions are (1) a holistic view of life, blending the sacred and the secular in one spiritual universe, and (2) a conception of God as almighty and sovereign.[48]

Black womanist theologians such as Katie Cannon, Jacquelyn Grant, and Delores Williams argue for the inclusion of African American women's experience, spirituality, biography, and literature in theological discourse. Their declaration of African American women's experience as a source for theological interpretation may mean that African American women's experience ought to be regarded as a starting point for a new theological enterprise separate from both black theology and white feminist theology. Grant says:

> I maintain that Black women scholars should follow Alice Walker by describing our theological activity as "womanist theology." The term "womanist" refers to Black women's experiences. It accents, as Walker says, our being responsible, in charge, outrageous, courageous and audacious enough to demand the right to think theologically and to do it independently of both white and Black men and white women.[49]

Is African American women's experience the foundation for a theological enterprise completely separate from black theology, or is it a source for correcting and enriching black theology and thus serving as loci for an ancillary discussion within black theology? Womanists answer both ways. While some womanists perceive their work as a form of black theology, some do not.

Tradition, as a source of theology, is understood to mean several things. James Cone defines tradition as the history of Christian thought and practice, that is, the story of how Christians at various times in history understood the gospel of Jesus Christ as recounted in the Bible.[50] However, he is not completely accepting or uncriti-

47. Wilmore, *Black Religion and Black Radicalism*, 2d ed., 235–40.

48. Cecil W. Cone, *The Identity Crisis in Black Theology* (Nashville: African Methodist Episcopal Church, 1975), 28–29.

49. Jacquelyn Grant, *White Woman's Christ and Black Woman's Jesus: Feminist Christology and Womanist Response* (Atlanta: Scholars Press, 1989), 209.

50. Cone, *A Black Theology of Liberation*, Twentieth Anniversary Edition, 33.

cal of the history of Christian thought and practice. According to Cone, black theology must be critical of the history of Western Christianity, especially after the fourth century when the church became a sanctioner rather than a moral critic and transformer of society.[51] The aspect of tradition that is of greatest significance to Evans is the worship traditions of African American churches.[52]

Revelation — God's self-disclosure — is recognized as the principal source of black theology. For black theologians in the Black Hermeneutical School, God's self-disclosure is not antithetical to African American history and culture. Though distinguishable, revelation and the experience of blackness are bound together into one reality, according to James Cone.[53] God reveals Godself in African American history.[54] African Americans have come to know and understand God through the manner in and conditions under which they have lived. They have come to know God especially through their struggles against oppression. Black theologians believe that this revelation of the divine nature in black life and culture is part and parcel of God's revelation elsewhere, such as in scripture and among other peoples' experiences.[55] James Cone says:

> God is found not only among blacks in North America but also in Latin America; not only among Christians in Africa but also among devotees of African traditional religions on that continent. God is found not only in European history but also in the history of Asia long before the arrival of European missionaries. . . . God has been known and experienced in many ways. . . . Because we have an imperfect grasp of divine reality, we must not regard our limited vision as absolute.[56]

Cone is aware that while God reveals Godself in African American life, history, and culture, God reveals Godself to other peoples elsewhere.

The Bible is an important source for black theology. Roberts contends that black theological interpretation starts with, and in the end

---

51. Ibid.
52. Evans, *We Have Been Believers*, 27–28.
53. Cone, *God of the Oppressed*, 35.
54. Evans, *We Have Been Believers*, 11.
55. Cone, *For My People*, 205–6.
56. Ibid.

seeks to be faithful to, the Bible.[57] Cecil Cone and Major Jones agree that the Bible is a principal source of black theology.[58] According to James Cone, the Bible is an indispensable witness to God's revelation,[59] but, he does not regard the Bible as an infallible witness. The Bible is not to be taken, in all points, literally.[60] Instead, the Bible occupies an important role for its model of revelation. The biblical model of God's revelation enables persons in the present generation to identify God's activity in the world.

James Evans contends that the Bible is "the primary, though not exclusive, conduit of the community's understanding of God's being and acts."[61] Like James Cone, Evans is aware that in the history of Christianity the Bible has been used both to suppress and to liberate African Americans. The Bible was used to denigrate Africans and sanction their enslavement. Evans asserts that "from about 1772 until 1850 the Bible was the primary source of authority and legitimation for the enslavement of Africans."[62] African American slaves countered the biblical interpretations of their captors with an alternative reading of the Bible that laid a foundation for African Americans' struggle for political emancipation, assertion of cultural integrity and racial pride, and affirmation of personal self-worth.[63]

As a source of black theology, reason is subordinate to revelation. According to Evans, whether understood as either Western philosophy or prevailing canons of rationality, reason is not a necessary source of black theology.[64] African American Christians and theologians are not obligated to use philosophy or adhere strictly to prevailing academic canons of rationality and truth. For Evans, "reason" seems to be a broad covering term that refers to human intellect or knowledge in the pursuit of or demonstration of truth about God. He thinks that reason stands in contrast to God's own self-disclosure, as African Americans have come to know God in their experiences.

Cecil Cone does not strictly prohibit use of Western intellectual

---

57. Roberts, *Black Theology Today*, 27.
58. Cone, *Identity Crisis in Black Theology*, 35; Jones, *The Color of God*, 2.
59. Cone, *A Black Theology of Liberation*, Twentieth Anniversary Edition, 31.
60. Ibid.
61. Evans, *We Have Been Believers*, 33.
62. Ibid., 35.
63. Ibid., 40–44.
64. Ibid., 28–29.

traditions and fields of knowledge. However, he cautions black theologians against using most fields of Western intellectual activity. He believes that if white people developed these fields without giving proper regard to the religion and experiences of African Americans, then a large part of the methods and findings in these areas of knowledge are inappropriate or irrelevant to black theology.[65] His belief is grounded in the suspicion that the absence of black participation distorts these areas of knowledge.

Dwight Hopkins's views on reason as a source of black theology are similar to Cecil Cone's and James Evans's. According to Hopkins, black theology must rely on its own indigenous sources.[66] However, this reliance is not exclusive. While black indigenous sources are the foundation of black theology, other sources may be added if they are compatible with and useful in accomplishing the tasks of black theology. Believing that the black theologian is free to utilize various sources of information, provided that the information gained is not contradictory to indigenous sources, black theologians use other disciplines and methodological perspectives. Hopkins, for example, identifies four academic disciplines of special use to black theology: political economy, biblical criticism, literary criticism, and comparative religions.[67]

From an altogether different approach than James Evans's, Cecil Cone's, and Dwight Hopkins's, J. Deotis Roberts subordinates reason to revelation. For example, in the case of black suffering, Roberts contends that reason is limited in its capacity to understand and overcome suffering. He says:

> Philosophers and theologians have never been able to find the ultimate solution to this enigma within a mystery. Many a thoughtful person has wrecked his faith on this reef. Christians have been enlightened by their reflection upon the problem of evil, but it has been their faith in the love, justice and power of God which has enabled them to conquer and transcend the power of evil in their lives.[68]

---

65. Cone, *Identity Crisis in Black Theology*, 18.
66. Dwight N. Hopkins, "Black Theology and a Second Generation," in *Black Theology: A Documentary History, Volume Two: 1980–1992*, ed. Cone and Wilmore, 62–63.
67. Ibid., 64–65.
68. Roberts, *Black Theology Today*, 37.

Convinced of the superiority of faith over reason, Roberts remains committed to a circle of faith. His perspective, however, has not prohibited him from tapping a wide variety of sources. He is not opposed to reason in interpreting matters of faith. He says:

> A theologian, as theologian, must work with conviction, I believe, out of a belief-system. Faith should have first place, therefore, but there should also be a quest for understanding what one believes. This means that theological assertions should be carefully and critically examined by means of all our logical and critical powers.[69]

Describing his quest to understand black Christian faith, he tells of the forms of reason that he has used. He says:

> My theological perspective has grown in relation to several academic disciplines. It began with philosophy and biblical studies. It now includes world religions, ethics, literature, and the social sciences, among other fields of investigation. This broad excursion into various fields of knowledge is useful in reflection upon the African American religious heritage.[70]

## NORM

The norm of black theology in the Black Hermeneutical School is a nonfoundationalist conception of Christian faith. By nonfoundationalist I mean that theologians in this school do not think that Christian faith requires explanation, grounding, or defense in sources external to the faith of the community or to the theologian's own faith. In the Black Hermeneutical School, conceptions of Christian faith are biblical, communal, and personal.

Black theologians in the Black Hermeneutical School assert that Christian faith has its own unique rationality and logic. According to James Cone:

> Christian theologians must admit that their logic is not the same as other forms of rational discourse. The coming of God in Jesus

69. Ibid., 42.
70. Roberts, *Prophethood of Black Believers,* xi.

breaks open history and thereby creates an experience of truth-encounter that makes us talk in ways often not understandable to those who have not had the experience.[71]

Agreeing with him, James Evans contends that conceptions of God are legitimated and justified in the experiences of specific Christian communities.[72] In black theology the concept of God is legitimated and justified in the experiences of African Americans as well. According to Evans, languages are characterized by their own sets of rules. He concludes that if African Americans have a distinct way of communicating their experiences, then their religious language has its own rules of logic and modes of understanding.

Gayraud Wilmore contends that theological "propositions and presuppositions need to be tested by the people's faith."[73] Wilmore is not suggesting with this statement that whatever the people say is always right. The theologian must sometimes take a stand on what he or she thinks personally that Christian faith is. At any rate, Wilmore maintains that black theology must be compatible with the faith and experiences of typical black church members. Similarly, James Cone says that the real test of whether any theological affirmation is appropriate to black theology depends on that affirmation's compatibility with what black people believe to be truthful on the basis of their struggle against oppression.[74] Black theology must mirror the truth professed in the community of the faithful. Wilmore's emphasis on the normative quality of the faith of the community is based on "the assumption that the gospel itself stands in judgment upon all human knowledge and endeavor and that [it must be permitted] to authenticate [the] academic enterprise."[75] The gospel or Christian faith is precisely the source that inspires academic black theology's departure from the canons of university scholarship, according to James Evans.[76] Evans says that "the norm of Christian theological affirmations is the

---

71. Cone, *God of the Oppressed,* 191.
72. Evans, *We Have Been Believers,* 66.
73. Gayraud S. Wilmore, General Introduction to *African American Religious Studies,* xviii.
74. Cone, *God of the Oppressed,* 252–53 n. 38.
75. Wilmore, General Introduction to *African American Religious Studies,* xvii–xviii.
76. James H. Evans, "Black Church Studies and the Theological Curriculum," in *African American Religious Studies,* ed. Gayraud S. Wilmore, 31.

acme of God's revelation in some notion of the identity and mission or the person and work of Jesus Christ."[77]

More than anyone else, James Cone attempts to explain how Christian faith — faith in Jesus Christ — functions as the norm of black theology. Cone emphasizes the need for a universalism in black theology that prevents it from becoming a mere ethnic particularism, racial ideology, and an uncritical acceptance and use of black sources.[78] He is not satisfied with a mere partial grasp of the truth. Cone says that "We can and must say something about the world that is not reducible to our own subjectivity."[79] "Humans must speak of the finite as if it were the ultimate."[80] As Cone says, the eventual aim of inquiry, our apprehension of truth, is to overcome or avoid imprisonment to subjectivity.[81] According to him, an individual overcomes simple subjectivity, the initial subjectivity of her perspective, when she achieves a vision of truth that is an aggregate of several perspectives. While this aggregate of perspectives may include some contribution from her own perspective, this aggregate is superior to her initial perspective. As one's perspective intersects and overlaps with the perspectives of others, one achieves transcendence — a vision beyond one's initial subjective point of view.[82] This newfound truth in this enlarged perspective must be reflected in and also compatible with Ultimate Truth.

## FAITH IN CHRIST

James Cone's claim that Jesus Christ is the norm of black theology presupposes a form of "perspective realism."[83] In the context of his work, perspective realism is the belief that truth is seen from particular points of view and speculation does not contribute to an accurate perception of the truth. In other words, truth is not a product of the human mind. Truth is something external to humans but from the

77. Evans, *We Have Been Believers*, 29.

78. Cone, "An Interpretation of the Debate among Black Theologians," Epilogue to *Black Theology: A Documentary History, 1966–1979*, ed. Cone and Wilmore, 618–20.

79. Cone, *God of the Oppressed*, 102.

80. Cone, *A Black Theology of Liberation*, Twentieth Anniversary Edition, 78.

81. Cone, *God of the Oppressed*, 107.

82. Ibid., 102–3.

83. The term "perspective realism" is coined and explained in Evander B. McGilvary, *Toward a Perspective Realism*, The Paul Carus Lectures, 1939, ed. Albert G. Ramsperger (LaSalle, Ill.: Open Court, 1956).

proper perspective we may apprehend it. But the individual, as well as any group to which she belongs, apprehends truth only partially. The individual perceiver's life situation is a condition for vision, but she neither adds nor takes away anything from the truth. Thus, a perspective is not an act or creation of the perceiver. In "seeing" the truth, the individual performs no action that can affect the truth perceived.

As truth, Jesus Christ is objective. He is totally other. He stands in judgment over all statements about truth.[84] He initiates encounters with human beings and causes them to seek transcendence.[85] He compels people who perceive him to look beyond their own perspectives and find witnesses to the same truth he reveals in their social contexts. However, truth, in whatever source revealed, will always be in favor and support of black liberation. The objectivity in Jesus Christ is not characterized by dispassion or disinterest. The proof of objectivity is in theological interpretations of the person and work of Jesus Christ that sustain and become the very soul of black liberation.[86]

As the truth, Christ is not affected by our subjective states nor is his identity limited to any historical manifestation.[87] Persons are not free to make Christ whom they wish for him to be. Persons are incapable of contributing anything to Christ's identity. If Christ is to be viewed accurately, then that view must be through whatever means he chooses to reveal himself. James Cone thinks saying that Jesus is black is appropriate, because of his identification with the oppressed who are today black. While this and other present and past manifestations of Jesus Christ are significant for our understanding of him, they do not exhaust his identity.[88]

Black theologians understand Jesus' blackness in various ways. For James Cone, Jacquelyn Grant, and Kelly Douglas, Jesus' blackness is ontological. For J. Deotis Roberts, Jesus' blackness is mythical. For Dwight Hopkins, Jesus' blackness is spiritual. For Albert Cleage, Jesus' blackness is physical, a matter of historical fact. Cleage says:

> When I say Jesus was black, that Jesus was the black Messiah, I'm not saying "Wouldn't it be nice if Jesus was black?" or "Let's

84. Cone, *God of the Oppressed*, 33.
85. Ibid., 109, 110.
86. Cone, *A Black Theology of Liberation*, Twentieth Anniversary Edition, 38.
87. Ibid., 119.
88. Cone, *God of the Oppressed*, 126.

pretend that Jesus was black" or "It's necessary psychologically for us to believe that Jesus was black." I'm saying that Jesus WAS black.[89]

Cleage bases his assertion of Jesus' blackness on the New Testament genealogy of Jesus in the book of Matthew and Old Testament genealogies and tables of nations which, he contends, name individuals and groups that are black racially. His so-called historically accurate portrait presents Jesus as "a revolutionary black leader, a Zealot, seeking to lead a Black Nation to freedom."[90]

For James Cone, Jesus' blackness is an ontological symbol, "a visible reality which best describes what oppression means in America."[91] The blackness of Jesus reveals God's solidarity with the oppressed who, in the United States, happen to be black. Cone is open to other ontological symbols of God's solidarity with the oppressed. For him, "mother" or "female," "rice," "red," to name a few, are capable of representing God's solidarity with the oppressed. He says:

> I am more convinced today than I was during the 1960s that the God of the Christian gospel can be known only in the communities of the oppressed who are struggling for justice in a world that has no place for them. I still believe that "God is Black" in the sense that God's identity is found in the faces of those who are exploited and humiliated because of their color. But I also believe that "God is mother," "rice," "red," and a host of other things that give life to those whom society condemns to death. "Black," "mother," "rice," and "red" give concreteness to God's life-giving presence in the world and remind us that the universality of God is found in the particularity of the suffering poor.[92]

He goes on to say, "God's truth comes in many colors and is revealed in many cultures, histories, and unexpected places."[93] For Cone, Jesus

---

89. Albert B. Cleage Jr., quoted in Alex Poinsett, "The Quest for a Black Christ," *Ebony* 24, no. 5 (March 1969): 176.

90. Albert B. Cleage Jr., *Black Christian Nationalism* (New York: William Morrow & Co., 1972), 4.

91. James H. Cone, *Black Theology and Black Power,* Twentieth Anniversary Edition (New York: Seabury Press, 1969; San Francisco: HarperCollins, 1989), 27.

92. James H. Cone, "God Is Black," in *Lift Every Voice: Constructing Christian Theologies from the Underside,* ed. Susan Brooks Thistlethwaite and Mary Potter Engel (San Francisco: Harper & Row, 1990), 83.

93. Cone, *For My People,* 206.

is unique to a religion, Christianity, but he is not normative for all religions. He does not believe that all encounters with God are constituted by or explainable in terms of the Christ-event. Jesus is of universal significance in that he can be related to other religions and secular movements that manifest the presence of God in liberating activity.

According to Jacquelyn Grant, a truly liberating ontological symbol of Christ for the oppressed in the United States is the image of the black woman.[94] She shares James Cone's conception of Jesus' ontological blackness, albeit with some modifications. She asserts that Jesus is black and female rather than male, as Cone had assumed early in his theological career. Against any Christians or theologians, white or African American, placing major emphasis on Jesus' masculinity, Grant argues that maleness is not an essential property in Jesus. In other words, his being male communicates nothing of religious or theological significance. Instead, she says, "The most significant events of Jesus Christ were the life and ministry, the crucifixion, and the resurrection."[95] According to her, these events are representative of God's liberating actions on behalf of the oppressed and the inspiration for them to seek freedom. After dispensing with maleness, she contends that the significant events of Jesus Christ were for the liberation of the least in human society. She says that, in our day, black women are the least among the least, the poorest of the poor, the most oppressed among the oppressed in the United States.[96]

Grant says that, for large numbers of black women, racism, classism, and sexism seriously diminish the quality of their lives. Because these three oppressive realities intersect in the lives of black women, Grant contends that the image of Christ as a black woman encourages black liberation theology to be holistic and thus focus on multiple forms of oppression.[97] According to her, the failure of black male theologians to develop holistic liberation theologies results from their limiting conceptions of Jesus' blackness to the problem of racism. In contrast, as

---

94. Grant, *White Woman's Christ and Black Woman's Jesus*, 220.

95. Jacquelyn Grant, "Womanist Theology: Black Women's Experience as a Source for Doing Theology, with Special Reference to Christology," in *Black Theology: A Documentary History, Volume Two: 1980–1992*, ed. Cone and Wilmore, 286.

96. Grant, *White Woman's Christ and Black Woman's Jesus*, 216.

97. Ibid., 2–3.

she contends, Jesus Christ as a black woman heightens awareness not only of racism but also the problems of classism and sexism.

For J. Deotis Roberts, Christ's representation as black or any other feature of other ethnic and social groups can only be mythical or symbolic.[98] However, the historical Jesus stands as the measure for all of these images of Christ. He contends that the black Christ is a way for African Americans to encounter God from their social and cultural position. For Roberts, as easily as Christ can be black, Christ can also be red, yellow, white, or female. However, this symbolism is not exempt from critical judgment. He says:

> For me, the Jesus of history is the Christ of faith. Christ is the center of God's revelation, but the circumference of God's salvific revelation is in all of creation and all of history and among all peoples. God is with us in Christ. God meets us in Christ where we are ethnically and culturally. God is Lord of *each* people and yet Lord of all. Christology is particular and, at the same time, universal.[99]

According to Roberts, while the black Christ is only a symbol or myth, he has profound meaning for black people. The black Christ makes the gospel direct and relevant to black people. The black Christ is an image that enables them to retrieve their dignity and pride and to have a sense of encounter with and worth before God.[100] Roberts contends that the black Christ points to an even greater work of God in the universal Christ. "The black Messiah liberates the black person. The universal Christ reconciles the black person with the rest of humankind."[101] So, for Roberts, if the black Christ, as well as any other ethnic or cultural images of Christ, is to be a genuine symbol, then it must direct the attention of African Americans not only to the improvement of their social condition but also to their improved relationships to other peoples.

Kelly Brown Douglas considers the black Christ to be a significant image in African American religion but points to its weaknesses and cautions against restriction of Christology to any one gender or eth-

---

98. Roberts, *Liberation and Reconciliation*, revised ed., 73.
99. J. Deotis Roberts, *Black Theology in Dialogue* (Philadelphia: Westminster Press, 1987), 41.
100. Roberts, *Liberation and Reconciliation*, revised ed., 72.
101. Ibid., 73.

nic group. With respect to the strengths of the black Christ, she calls attention to how the image affirms blackness physically and culturally, fosters self-esteem and pride, allows black people to see themselves in the divine nature, and thus fortifies their resolve for realization and fulfillment. Notwithstanding these qualities, the black Christ exhibits weaknesses of which Douglas points out five.[102]

First, the image of a black Christ may lead to an unconditional affirmation of blackness. Not all aspects and practices of black culture are sustaining and liberating. If not well defined, the image could hinder rather than facilitate liberation. Second, the image may focus no attention on oppression within African American churches and communities. Following from this second flaw, the image may lead, third, to a one-dimensional analysis of oppression, fixating on racism as the only barrier to liberation when in fact other barriers to liberation exist as well. Fourth, the black Christ enjoys only a limited acceptance in African American churches. Many black churches continue to display and revere images of a white Christ. Last, the black Christ is often portrayed as male and, as a result, compromises the value, equality, and contributions of women. Like Jacquelyn Grant, Douglas sees Christ as both black and female, a black woman.[103] She insists that Christ, symbolized as a black woman, provides a multidimensional analysis of oppression for the entire African American community.[104] However, as a committed womanist, she is open to — and argues that other people as well ought to be open to — the use of alternate depictions of Christ. She says, "Christ for the Black community can be woman but the presence of Christ is not restricted to Black women."[105]

For Dwight Hopkins, Jesus' blackness is metaphysical, which he expresses using the metaphor of spirit. He claims that God is the "spirit of liberation."[106] His intention is to avoid gender-specific terminology for talk about God. This metaphorical and doctrinal emphasis on spirit makes God gender-inclusive, according to Hopkins. Notwithstanding this approach, he contends that Jesus is the decisive revelation of God,

102. Kelly Brown Douglas, *The Black Christ* (Maryknoll, N.Y.: Orbis Books, 1994), 84–92.
103. Ibid., 108–9.
104. Ibid., 109.
105. Ibid., 110.
106. Hopkins, *Introducing Black Theology of Liberation,* 46.

this spirit of liberation, albeit the divine nature is manifest in various ways in many peoples' struggles for freedom and justice.[107]

## RELATED BELIEFS

The shared conviction of black theologians, however expressed, that Jesus Christ is black leads to three other beliefs that are normative for the Black Hermeneutical School: (1) the belief that God is black; (2) the belief that liberation is of infinite and unquestionable value; and (3) the belief that the black experience is *heilsgeschichte,* a part of sacred history. The black Christ mediates the character and intentions of God. James Cone says, "Jesus is not a human being for all persons, he is a human being for oppressed persons."[108] Because of Jesus' identification with the oppressed, Cone goes further to assert that God is a not a God for all peoples.[109] Just as Jesus is black, God is also black in that God is in solidarity with oppressed blacks. William R. Jones calls this belief in God's blackness or solidarity with the oppressed "black liberation theism." In the next chapter, I discuss Jones's criticism of black liberation theism.

James Evans explains God's blackness in terms of what he claims are two of God's principal attributes: impartiality and partiality. According to Evans, God is impartial in that "God [is] the universal parent of all humankind and . . . all people [are] created from the same dust."[110] God values God's creatures equally. For God's creatures, God wills justice. In situations of injustice, God becomes partial, according to Evans.[111] God takes sides with creatures who are oppressed in order to restore or achieve justice. Because African Americans are victims of injustice, God takes sides with them and champions their cause as God's own crusade for justice.[112]

When seen as the aim of God, liberation takes on a sacred quality for black theologians. Albert Cleage says, "Nothing is more sacred than

---

107. Dwight N. Hopkins, *Down, Up, and Over: Slave Religion and Black Theology* (Minneapolis: Fortress Press, 2000), 193. More so than men, women emphasize God as spirit — spirit of liberation, spirit of creation, spirit of life, and so on, according to Karen Baker-Fletcher, "God as Spirit: Womanist Perspectives on God," chap. 1, *My Sister, My Brother: Womanist and Xodus God-Talk* (Maryknoll, N.Y.: Orbis Books, 1997).
108. Cone, *A Black Theology of Liberation,* Twentieth Anniversary Edition, 85–86.
109. Ibid., 63.
110. Evans, *We Have Been Believers,* 67.
111. Ibid., 69.
112. Ibid., 71.

the liberation of Black people."[113] Anything that affirms or makes possible liberation is true. That which does not make liberation possible is rejected as false. Also, beliefs suspected of leading to logical contradictions are retained if they contribute to the cause of liberation. James Cone contends that black Christian faith need not be empirically verifiable in order to be true.[114] If black people believe in a proposition that contributes to their quest for liberation, then that proposition is true. According to Cleage, the achievement of liberation is the measure of all things. He says:

> If it supports the Liberation Struggle of Black People, then it is good. If it is in opposition to the Liberation Struggle of Black People, then it is bad. If it supports the Liberation Struggle of Black People, then it is moral. If it opposes the Liberation Struggle, then it is immoral. If it supports the Liberation Struggle of Black People, then it is the will of God. If it opposes the Liberation Struggle of Black People, then it is satanic.[115]

In essential agreement with Cleage, James Cone says:

> When the question is asked, "On what authority, in the last resort, do we base our claim that this or that doctrine is part of the Gospel and therefore true?" Black Theology must say: "If the doctrine is compatible with or enhances the drive for black freedom, then it is the gospel of Jesus Christ. If the doctrine is against or indifferent to the essence of blackness as expressed in Black Power, then it is the work of Antichrist."[116]

So, for Cone, as with Cleage, "all ideas which are opposed to the struggle for black self-determination or irrelevant to it must be rejected."[117]

Delores Williams rejects a basic, traditional doctrine like atonement because she believes it cannot advance black women's liberation. For Williams, a truly liberating image of Jesus Christ must dispense with

---

113. Cleage, *Black Christian Nationalism*, 9.
114. James H. Cone, *Speaking the Truth: Ecumenism, Liberation, and Black Theology* (Grand Rapids: Eerdmans, 1986), 13–15.
115. Cleage, *Black Christian Nationalism*, xviii–xix.
116. Cone, *Black Theology and Black Power*, Twentieth Anniversary Edition, 121.
117. Ibid., 120.

the traditional doctrine of atonement, the belief that humans are redeemed through Jesus' having innocently suffered violence, abuse, and
death at the hands of evil men. She is not denying the fact that Jesus
died in that manner. In her thinking, atonement places too much emphasis on Jesus' suffering and not enough on his visionary teachings.
Instead of Jesus' death, she contends that humankind is redeemed
through Jesus' ministerial vision of life. She says:

> Nothing is divine in the blood of the cross. . . . Jesus did not come
> to be a surrogate. Jesus came for life, to show humans a perfect
> vision of ministerial relation that humans had very little knowl-
> edge of. As Christians, black women cannot forget the cross, but
> neither can they glorify it. To do so is to glorify suffering and to
> render their exploitation sacred.[118]

For Williams, the oppressed are not motivated to overcome their sufferings when, in atonement, they see suffering glorified in Jesus Christ,
as if it was his suffering alone that results in redemption.

In belief that the black Christ discloses how God is at work in the
world, particularly in the lives of black people, James Cone contends
that the experiences and thoughts of black people cannot be overlooked, minimized, or denied in theological reflection. According to
him, in order for persons to relate effectively to and know God, they
must become black with God — that is, join in solidarity with oppressed blacks.[119] For Cone, the normativity of blackness is further
seen in how the sources for black theological reflection are treated.
For instance, the Bible, as a source for theology, is read deliberately
with the intention of producing a liberative effect in the lives of black
people. Later in my discussion on method in the Black Hermeneutical School, I talk about Cone's principle of hermeneutics for reading
the Bible.

James Cone's principle for biblical interpretation, however, makes
imperative that one's biblical and theological interpretation in black
theology demonstrate that liberation is the essential message of the
gospel of Jesus Christ. In the section on sources in the Black Hermeneutical School, I mentioned Cone's assertion that black experience is

---

118. Williams, *Sisters in the Wilderness,* 167.
119. Cone, *A Black Theology of Liberation,* Twentieth Anniversary Edition, 65.

a source of black theology. For him, the black experience is a medium through which other sources are appropriated. From the experiences of African Americans, he identifies sermons, prayers, religious and secular songs (e.g., spirituals and the blues), folktales, personal narratives, black literature, worship, and spirituality as sources for black theology.

## METHOD

In the Black Hermeneutical School, the method of black theology is hermeneutics. The forms of hermeneutics used are biblical hermeneutics, correlation, narrative criticism, and philosophical hermeneutics. These methods are not aimed at the discovery of new truth. Instead, they are aimed at the description and explanation of the experiences and faith claims of believing communities.

According to J. Deotis Roberts, the hermeneutics of black theology begins and ends with the Bible.[120] James Cone agrees with Roberts. Cone says that the Bible is the primary source of theological language and determines how other sources are used in black theology.[121] Roberts says that this focus on the Bible is characterized by (1) a universal vision that permits the contextualization of theology in all cultures, ethnic groups, and religions; (2) a commitment to human rights for all peoples; and (3) a sense of the connection between thought and action.[122] He contends that these tendencies, which characterize a black hermeneutics, permit black theology to expand upon the Bible in a way that makes the Bible relevant to the contemporary situation of African Americans and still meaningful to other peoples.

In response to the question, "How must the theologian read and appropriate the Bible?" James Cone answers by saying:

> The hermeneutical principle for an exegesis of the Scriptures is the revelation of God in Christ as the Liberator of the oppressed from social oppression and to political struggle, wherein the poor recognize that their fight against poverty and injustice is not only consistent with the gospel but is the gospel of Jesus Christ.[123]

---

120. Roberts, *Black Theology Today*, 27.
121. Cone, *Speaking the Truth*, 4.
122. Roberts, *Black Theology Today*, 28–29.
123. Cone, *God of the Oppressed*, 81–82.

If one reads the Bible in this way, four results should follow, according to Cone.[124] First, one's theology will address social and political conditions that are either a result of or symptomatic of oppression. Second, one's theology will become prophetic and thereby speak the truth of the gospel in a manner relevant to the plight of the oppressed and challenge systems of injustice. Third, because one is correlating the gospel to new situations, one's theology will advance beyond tradition or extend the gospel in new ways. One will say an old message in new ways. Fourth, one's theology will become a word of judgment against the oppressors or ruling class.

As mentioned earlier in the section on the content of black theology, Delores Williams contends that two traditions of biblical interpretation are present in African American religious communities: one emphasizing liberation and another emphasizing survival. According to Williams, the liberation tradition focuses on the liberation of the oppressed and shows God relating to males in the liberation struggle. James Cone's biblical hermeneutics falls into the category of the liberation tradition of biblical appropriation, according to Williams. The survival/quality-of-life tradition emphasizes God's immediate response to black people's present situation rather than their future liberation. God acts now to improve black people's quality of life and aids them in their struggle for survival.

The paradigm for this survival tradition, as mentioned earlier, is the Old Testament narrative on Hagar, the Egyptian slave of Abraham and Sarah, according to Delores Williams. However, the ethicist Cheryl Sanders uses the metaphor of exile to emphasize survival and quality of life. As Williams points out, God does not act to liberate Hagar. Instead, God acts to make possible her survival, improves her quality of life, and builds a community — a nation — from her son Ishmael, who was cast out with her from Abraham's house and turned into the wilderness. Williams finds a foundation for her womanist theology through her reading of the Hagar narrative. Williams sees parallels between Hagar's situation and "many African American women's predicament of poverty, sexual and economic exploitation, surrogacy, domestic violence, homelessness, rape, motherhood, single-parenting,

---

124. Ibid., 82–83.

ethnicity, and meetings with God."[125] Williams's interpretation of the Hagar narrative sets the parameters of her womanist theology and informs her critique of the traditional view of atonement, which she sees as promoting the exploitation of the innocent, those deserving no harm. Thus, for Williams, the survivalist tradition more than the liberationist tradition enables her to correlate Christianity, interpreted through the paradigm of Hagar's experience, and black women's experience.

Early into the black theological movement, James Cone asserted that black theology involved a critical correlation of sorts.[126] Black theologians of the Black Hermeneutical School understand the interpretive task of theology as a mediation between Christian faith and the changing conditions of African American life. Black theologians take the interpreted truth of Christianity and correlate it with interpretations of the contemporary culture and plight of African Americans.

Narrative criticism is a methodology based upon the conviction that the sources of black theology are stories — that is to say, expressed in narrative form.[127] According to James Evans, the norms governing narrative discourse are inherent in the stories themselves.[128] The type and structure of the stories determine how they are to be appropriated, what can be said to or done with them in theological reflection.

An example of philosophical hermeneutics is Dwight Hopkins's method of interpretation that he calls "rhythm."[129] His theory applies to a wide range of sources. Rhythm is a three-step process involving: (1) solidarity with the poor (faith in, commitment to, worship with, and work with the African American poor); (2) critical reflection on actual beliefs and practices of liberation in both religious and secular settings (which can be mediated through a variety of sources); and (3) applying theological insights gained in step 2 for improving life for the poor. Whether or not the spirit of liberation is truly present determines the validity and accuracy of each step. Also, each step must have as a guide attention to context (historical, social, political, cultural, linguistic, etc.), content (sources available for interpretation),

---

125. Williams, *Sisters in the Wilderness*, 5–6.
126. Cone, *God of the Oppressed*, 16–17; idem, *A Black Theology of Liberation*, Twentieth Anniversary Edition, xix, 4–5, 21–23.
127. Cone, *God of the Oppressed*, 54.
128. Evans, *We Have Been Believers*, 31.
129. Hopkins, *Introducing Black Theology of Liberation*, 47–48.

construction (the challenge of presenting new or alternative views of reality), and commitment (solidarity with the poor).

## GOAL

The goal of black theology follows or adheres closely to its declared content. In the Black Hermeneutical School, the goal of black theology is moral and ethical action that leads to liberation.[130] The goal of black theology is not the resolution of esoteric issues of concern only to academicians. Black theology's goal is liberation in the real world. The focus of black theology is on life, especially when it must be lived under the worst conditions. James Cone says, "Christians believe that their faith has something to say about this world and about the human beings in it — something that can make a decisive difference in the quality of life. It is therefore the task of theology to demonstrate the difference that the gospel can and does make in human lives, using the resources of the scriptures and traditions of the churches as well as other modern tools of social, historical, cultural, economic, and philosophical analysis."[131]

Eschatology and virtue theory serve as sources of norms for moral and ethical action. As the vision of a new social order, eschatology is intended to inspire hope in persons and motivate them to act. Gayraud Wilmore says that this vision is "the criterion of the present world, a model or perfection which stands in judgment upon it."[132] James Evans adds that the vision represents hope in the form of new possibilities for the oppressed and disciplines them in the pursuit to realize these possibilities. Major Jones writes that eschatological vision of a just society assures the oppressed of at least three things: (1) that something better exists for them than a life of oppression, (2) that tyranny has limits, and (3) that no effort toward realizing of the vision is in vain.[133] According to Evans, "[Eschatology] makes every historical gain only penultimate.... [T]he eschatological vision will not let the Christian settle for anything less than the perfect reign of God."[134] The vision

130. Evans, *We Have Been Believers*, 7.
131. Cone, *For My People*, 28–29.
132. Wilmore, *Last Things First*, 83.
133. Major J. Jones, *Christian Ethics for a Black Theology* (Nashville: Abingdon Press, 1974), 191.
134. Evans, *We Have Been Believers*, 152.

"prevents momentary failures from becoming permanent defeats."[135] More than a simple vision of possibilities, eschatology is a vision of a certain end. Whatever one has failed to achieve at the moment does not alter the end of human history.

James Cone contends that an eschatological vision capable of moving persons to moral and ethical action in pursuit of black liberation must exemplify at least six features.[136] First, the vision must emphasize black unity and black self-love. For Cone, black liberation begins with black racial cooperation — that is, how well blacks treat each other and work among themselves to improve their own condition. Second, the vision must hold out the possibility of blacks forming coalitions with whites, but strict emphasis must be placed on the timing of interracial coalition building. Such coalitions should emerge only after black unity has been achieved and blacks strike their own synthesis between the best in integrationist and nationalist philosophies, which Cone asserts are the two principal approaches that African Americans have taken to white racism.

Third, the vision must emphasize gender equality among African Americans. Fourth, the vision must emphasize democratic socialism, affirming individual freedom and the right of each person to access the goods, services, and benefits of membership in American society. Fifth, the vision must emphasize the connection between the black freedom struggle in the United States and the plight of oppressed peoples throughout the world. In emphasizing these connections, Cone believes that African Americans will find the motivation to form coalitions with other oppressed peoples. Last, the vision must simultaneously affirm the best in black religion and respect the religions of other oppressed peoples. For Cone, this affirmation and respect are made possible by maintaining a notion of general revelation, as mentioned earlier in the chapter section on sources of black theology. God's revelation is *heilsgeschichte* — that is, mighty acts in human history, not just in the experiences of Christians.

In James Cone's attempt to synthesize integrationism and nationalism, as espoused by Martin Luther King Jr. and Malcolm X, respectively, he develops a theory of virtue for black liberation ethics.

---

135. Ibid., 153.
136. Cone, *For My People*, 202–5.

He identifies nine strengths exemplified by King and Malcolm.[137] (1) Each shows pride in his blackness. (2) King excelled greatly in developing political strategies to change the sociopolitical relations between blacks and whites. (3) Each achieved a critique of American Christianity, King as an internal critic and Malcolm as an external critic. (4) Each showed leadership qualities such as courage, intelligence, and dedication. (5) Both men were self-critical and humble. (6) Each made courageous decisions on violence. King rejected violence and recognized nonviolent direct action as the most practical form of militancy. Malcolm emphasized the need for self-defense in order to protect African Americans' lives, property, and institutions against white violence. (7) Each combined militancy with humor and irony, being serious-minded but able to laugh when under intense pressures. (8) Both men were in solidarity with the poorest of blacks. (9) Both men linked the black freedom movement in the United States to other liberation movements in the world. The weaknesses that Cone sees in King and Malcolm are in each one's chauvinism and oversight of sexism and classism as major problems.[138]

J. Deotis Roberts and Major Jones dispute Cone's view that violence, in the form of self-defense, is moral or ethical for Christians. Roberts contends that "violence is inconsistent with Christian ethics."[139] He says, "If reconciliation is a proper goal, and I am convinced that it is, then violence that destroys the one who is party to the reconciliation is not a good means. There can be no reconciliation between the dead — at least not in this life."[140] Jones contends that, for Christians, the sanctity of human life is absolute. He says about Jesus, "He regarded life so highly that he chose rather to give up his own life."[141] Neither Jesus nor his disciples retaliated against nor killed people who were oppressing them. Under no circumstances is killing permissible. According to Jones, a person who accepts violence must also acknowledge that violence may result in death. Since death by violence compromises the sacredness of human life, one must reject violence.

---

137. Cone, *Martin and Malcolm and America*, 288–314.
138. Ibid., 274, 276.
139. Roberts, *Liberation and Reconciliation*, revised ed., 102.
140. Ibid., 103.
141. Jones, *Christian Ethics for a Black Theology*, 171.

Jesus is a model of virtue for Albert Cleage, but his view of Jesus is different than Major Jones's. For Cleage, Jesus is the black Messiah. As the black Messiah, according to Cleage, Jesus taught and exemplified in his life the virtues of black solidarity, black self-love, sacrifice, commitment, and discipline.[142] Jesus' life and teachings stress rejecting individualism and sacrificing oneself, one's personal interests, and if necessary, one's life for the liberation of the black nation. Cleage sees in the sacrament of Holy Communion the virtues exemplified and made sacred by Jesus and which black Christians must express also. He says:

> the broken bread is the symbol that we are willing as individuals to sacrifice ourselves for the Nation. The wine is the symbol that we're willing to shed our blood for the Nation. So when we come together, it's as though we were around a table united, a people, a Nation. And we are saying in our participation, in the sacrament of Holy Communion, "I'm a part of the Nation. I accept this sacrifice which the Black Messiah made as the symbolic sacrifice which I'm willing to make that the Nation may be built, that it may grow, that it may have power. I'm willing."[143]

Womanist theologians also look to exemplary personalities for moral values and models for ethical action. Jacquelyn Grant says, "Womanist just means *being* and *acting* out who you are."[144] Womanism is black women asserting their freedom and capacity for self-determination and demonstrating commitment and concern for the liberation of oppressed African Americans. According to Grant, women best modeling womanism include Sojourner Truth, Jarena Lee, Amanda Berry Smith, Ida B. Wells, Mary Church Terrell, Mary McLeod Bethune, and Fannie Lou Hamer.[145] In addition to the women named by Grant, womanist theologians also admire Harriet Tubman, Anna Julia Cooper, and Zora Neale Hurston. The lives of these African American women become texts and normative guides for a contemporary understanding of womanism and how it is best lived out. Womanist ethicists who are

---

142. Cleage, *Black Christian Nationalism,* xiii, 25–27.
143. Albert B. Cleage Jr., *The Black Messiah* (New York: Sheed and Ward, 1969; reprinted, Trenton, N.J.: Africa World Press, 1989), 32–33.
144. Grant, *White Woman's Christ and Black Woman's Jesus,* 205.
145. Ibid.

emphasizing the moral imperatives of women's experience and spirituality and examining critically and proposing new practices in African American churches and communities include Katie Cannon, Toinette Eugene, Marcia Riggs, Cheryl Sanders, and Emilie Townes.

For black theologians in the Black Hermeneutical School, the black church plays a vital role in the achievement of black liberation. James Cones asserts that the vision of a new social order must come from the black church.[146] In other words, African American churches must be the first to construct and promote the vision. Albert Cleage claims that the Black Church must unite, free the minds, and strengthen the bodies of black people,[147] contending that only the black church has the potential capacity to mobilize the total black community for social change.[148] No other institution affects the lives of so many African Americans.

In order for African American churches to rise to the challenge of transforming American society, they must accomplish several tasks beforehand, according to James Cone.[149] He says that, first of all, black churches must stop spending inordinate amounts of their time and resources on organizational operations, such as conventions and the construction and maintenance of splendid worship facilities. Second, black churches must become more critical of white American religion and culture. They must become more aware of religious ideas and cultural practices that contribute to the oppression of black people. Third, they must give attention to the development of their own theology in liturgy, creeds, and other documents. If they do not do it, no one else will. Fourth, leaders in black churches must become more accountable to their memberships by laboring for the improvement of their members' lives. Fifth, black churches must achieve and maintain an ecumenism characterized by cooperation across denominational lines. Sixth, black churches must eradicate sexism and other forms of discrimination from within their own institutional domains.

For womanist theologians, ecclesiastical change with respect to the eradication of sexism is a primary aim.[150] Kelly Douglas con-

---

146. Cone, *For My People,* 201.
147. Cleage, *The Black Messiah,* 20.
148. Cleage, *Black Christian Nationalism,* 201.
149. Cone, *My Soul Looks Back,* 88–92.
150. Peter J. Paris, "From Womanist Thought to Womanist Action," *Journal of Feminist Studies in Religion* 9 (spring–fall 1993): 115.

tends that African American churches need to reassess their views on human sexuality if they are to be at the forefront of liberation. Last, black churches must work to build solidarity and cooperation between African Americans and other groups of oppressed peoples.

J. Deotis Roberts's concern has been for African American churches to develop viable ministries. His conviction is that black churches can play an important role in strengthening black families. In Roberts's opinion, the ministry of black churches must consist of support to single parents, socializing males for greater involvement and responsibility in their families, building self-esteem especially in black children, and working to transform (or reform) institutional practices in American society that adversely affect black families.[151] Roberts does not deal only with the topic of ministry to families. He contends that the black church's ministry must be holistic — that is, priestly in its compassion toward and care for those in need, prophetic in its challenge to injustice and its example of an ethical lifestyle, and public in its engagement with and activity to combat evil in the world.[152]

This holistic type of ministry should result in activities and emphases such as Christian moral and spiritual education, the nurturing and socialization of youth, organized protest, pastoral care, meaningful participation of women in leadership roles for so long monopolized by men, financial accountability, the encouragement and undertaking of ventures in economic cooperation and development in black communities, mobilization of persons for involvement in political elections, and the maintaining of quality, uplifting worship services where people have a sense of God's presence.

## SUMMARY

Katie Cannon, Albert Cleage, Cecil Cone, James Cone, Kelly Brown Douglas, James Evans, Jacquelyn Grant, Dwight Hopkins, Major Jones, Olin Moyd, J. Deotis Roberts, Delores Williams, and Gayraud Wilmore's shared methodological perspective is evident in how they define the tasks, content, sources, norm, method, and goal of black theology. With varying degrees of emphasis, these theologies assert

---

151. J. Deotis Roberts, *Roots of a Black Future: Family and Church* (Philadelphia: Westminster Press, 1980), 119–32.

152. Roberts, *Prophethood of Black Believers,* 2–5.

that the tasks of black theology are description, analysis, evaluation, explanation, construction, and revision. Evans prefers to call the task of revision "deconstruction." Cannon, Douglas, and Williams place special emphasis on the tasks of theology and ethics for womanists.

All thinkers affirm that the content or central theme of black theology is liberation. They define liberation using the Bible and black folk stories that exemplify a determination for freedom. Using the Bible, Roberts, Jones, Moyd, and Williams relate liberation to other themes such as reconciliation, hope, redemption, and survival.

Sources of black theology are principally revelation; the Bible; black experience, spirituality, history, and culture; and reason when it is compatible with revelation.

The norm of black theology is nonfoundationalist (i.e., biblical, communal, and personal) conceptions of Christian faith that center around Jesus Christ as the black Messiah. The blackness of Jesus Christ is conceived in several ways: historically or physically (by Cleage), ontologically (by J. Cone, Grant, and Douglas), mythically (by Roberts), and pneumatologically (by Hopkins). However expressed, belief in the blackness of Jesus Christ leads to three other beliefs that have normative quality: (1) the belief that God is black, that is, in solidarity with African Americans and will liberate them; (2) the belief that liberation is of infinite and unquestionable value; and (3) the belief that the black experience is *heilsgeschichte*, a part of sacred history. The experiences of African Americans are imbued with a degree of authority. Although supposedly a source of black theology, black experience is the medium through which other sources are appropriated. The truth of ideas and doctrines is judged against how well they contribute to the liberation of oppressed African Americans.

The methods of the Black Hermeneutical School are hermeneutical. Methods used are biblical hermeneutics, correlation of interpretations of the gospel of Jesus Christ with assessments of contemporary situations, narrative criticism of black folk stories, and philosophical hermeneutics.

The goal of black theology is moral and ethical action leading to liberation. The black church is recognized as the major institution from which black liberation is launched and maintained. In order to make the black church more viable in terms of liberation, black theologians argue for changes in its institutional practices and the creation of ministries that will positively impact the lives of oppressed African Americans. Through the doctrine of eschatology and virtue theory based on the lives of exemplary individuals in the black liberation struggle, such as the black Christ, Martin Luther King Jr., Malcolm X, Sojourner Truth, Harriet Tubman, and so forth, black theologians identify principles for moral and ethical action.

# CHAPTER THREE

# The Black Philosophical School

**I**N CRITICISM OF THE THEODICIES of popular black theologians, namely, James Cone, Albert Cleage, Major Jones, Joseph Washington, and J. Deotis Roberts, William R. Jones wrote his book *Is God a White Racist?* (1973) with the intention of suggesting an interpretive forum for future debate in academic black theology.[1] He self-consciously charted a new intellectual course for scholars interested in the interpretation of African American religion. Besides taking a new approach to and creating a new forum for conversations in black theology, his book marked the entry of philosophers of religion and the use of philosophy in academic black theology. Evident in his book is an extensive use of insights gained from humanism, philosophical analysis, and logical argument.

In a 1978 issue of *Philosophical Forum* devoted to the theme of "Philosophy and the Black Experience," which was explored earlier in a 1973 conference under the same title at Tuskegee Institute, Jones defines "black philosophy" as an ethnic approach to a discipline.[2] The term "black" is not a biological classification but rather is indicative of a distinct cultural grouping. "Black" is a social, political, and cultural construct. Jones goes on to say that:

> One must recognize that precisely because of their situation in America as an oppressed racial minority, the history and culture of blacks have been marked by the factor of race. For this reason it is materially impossible to comprehend the black experience and ignore the racial factor, but this is a consequence of the historical context rather than the inner logic of a black philosophy. A

---

1. William R. Jones, *Is God a White Racist? A Preamble to Black Theology* (Garden City, N.Y.: Doubleday, Anchor Press, 1973), 203.
2. William R. Jones, "The Legitimacy and Necessity of Black Philosophy: Some Preliminary Considerations," *Philosophical Forum* 9 (winter–spring 1977–78): 149.

black philosophy is in no way obliged to make race its organizing principle.[3]

As Jones argues, understanding the history and culture of African Americans, and other American ethnic groups as well, is impossible without resorting to the issue of race and its impact on the life and thought of all Americans.

In addition to the relevance of an ethnic approach in response to the impact of race on American life, Jones maintains that black philosophy is both legitimate and necessary by virtue of what he sees as the particularism inherent to philosophy.[4] Jones contends that if philosophy, or theology for that matter, is to provide and examine descriptions of reality, then philosophers must recognize that reality cannot be grasped in one viewpoint alone. An enriched understanding of reality requires the testimony of several perspectives.[5] Philosophy therefore requires investigation from several perspectives in order to achieve its task. According to Jones, the perspective of African Americans merits consideration because it, like any other perspective, may serve as a point from which to launch inquiry.

Also in the same 1978 issue of *Philosophical Forum*, Cornel West defines black philosophy, which he prefers to call "Afro-American philosophy," as "the interpretation of Afro-American history, highlighting the cultural heritage and political struggles, which provide desirable norms that should regulate responses to particular challenges presently confronting Afro-Americans."[6] In essential agreement with Jones, he does not consider black philosophy to be a separate discipline. He thinks that projects to create or demonstrate a uniquely "black epistemology," "black ontology," or "black conceptions of space and time," because they adopt categories in Cartesian philosophy and fill these categories with "black" content, are "confused, misguided, and will prove to be unproductive."[7]

For West, "Afro-American philosophy is the application of philosophical techniques of interpretation and justification to the Afro-

---

3. Ibid., 152.
4. Ibid., 155.
5. Ibid., 156.
6. Cornel West, "Philosophy and the Afro-American Experience," *Philosophical Forum* 9 (winter–spring 1977–78): 122–23.
7. Ibid., 144 n. 4.

American experience."[8] He further works out the meaning of black philosophy in his phrase and self-identification as an "Afro-American intellectual," a term that refers to the individual who deals with "areas of intellectual enterprise that focus needed critical attention upon all aspects of black existence" and to "the sociocultural location that grounds one's intellectual perspective upon a wide variety of political, philosophical, and religious problems and concerns."[9] The phenomena in African American history of concern to West include "religious doctrines, political ideologies, artistic expression and unconscious modes of behavior."[10] The domain of black philosophy is the total reality that constitutes African American people's existence. For West, as well as for Jones, this domain includes religion.

## THINKERS

In addition to William R. Jones and Cornel West, other thinkers in the Black Philosophical School include Anthony Pinn, Alice Walker, and Henry Young. Jones is a philosopher of religion, and Pinn is a scholar in religious studies. Both use humanism as a major philosophical source in the interpretation of African American religion. West is a philosopher of religion who locates himself within the African American humanist tradition but uses pragmatism as his major philosophical source. Walker's concept of womanism, adopted by a great many African American religion scholars, is a form of humanism. Young is a systematic theologian who uses process philosophy in his construction of black liberation theology. Young's, Walker's, and West's conceptions of God are compatible with Jones's description of humanocentric theism.

## TASKS

Thinkers in the Black Philosophical School accept the Black Hermeneutical School's assertion that the tasks of black theology are description, analysis, evaluation, explanation, construction, and revi-

---

8. Ibid., 123.
9. Cornel West, as interpreted by Michael E. Dyson, *Reflecting Black: African American Cultural Criticism* (Minneapolis: University of Minnesota Press, 1993), 284.
10. West, "Philosophy and the Afro-American Experience," 123.

sion. The Black Philosophical School places great emphasis on the task of revision. For thinkers in the Black Philosophical School, the criticism and reconstruction of ideas is most crucial for the achievement of liberation. William R. Jones prefers to call the task of revision "gnosiological conversion."

In *Prophesy Deliverance!* Cornel West names five tasks constituting his constructive work in black liberation theology.[11] His first declared task is to offer a new self-understanding of African American experience. In other words, this task describes African American experience so as to display its complexity and richness. He wants to demonstrate that African American culture is not monolithic but heterogeneous — made up of several traditions of thought and practice. His second task is to investigate the metaphors, categories, and norms that shape and mold white racism. West's third task is to describe and evaluate African American responses to white racism. His fourth task is to demonstrate the compatibility between African American Christian thought and Marxist social philosophy. His motive here is to name or be more explicit about the institutions and practices in American society that result in oppression. Last, West's fifth task, and the goal to which all other tasks are directed, is to make practical suggestions on how liberation can be achieved.

From William R. Jones's understanding of normal academic disciplinary development, he identifies the tasks of black theology. Jones sees black theology progressing along three stages. He contends that these three stages are possible in any academic discipline. The three stages are legitimation, critical expansion, and systematic construction.[12]

In the phase of legitimation, black theologians assume the task of demonstrating that black theology is a distinct and irreducible area of study. According to Jones, black theologians accomplish legitimacy through two interrelated, overlapping strategies.[13] First, black theologians attempt to demonstrate the legitimacy of their work by attacking "white Christianity." They indict the Western tradition of Christianity and especially its established theologies for racism. As an example of

---

11. Cornel West, *Prophesy Deliverance! An Afro-American Revolutionary Christianity* (Philadelphia: Westminster Press, 1982), 22–23.

12. William R. Jones, "Toward an Interim Assessment of Black Theology," 515.

13. Ibid.

this indictment, he cites black theologians' attacks against religious art and symbols. Black theologians consider depictions of Jesus that are antithetical to the bodily, physical features and aesthetic sensibilities exhibited by African Americans to be indicative of white racism. Jones adds that, besides the defamation of white theologies, black theologians' attacks open an area for discussion on African Americans' unique understanding of Christianity and also on those beliefs and practices that would contribute to the liberation of oppressed African Americans. Thus, attacks on white theology are accompanied by an interest, on the part of black theologians, to explore the liberating aspects of African American religion.

A second way in which black theologians seek to accomplish legitimacy is by marking or blocking off, or what Jones calls "cornering," a specific theological turf for African Americans only. Black theologians may justify their work as an investigation of materials previously ignored by white theologians. They regard black sources such as spirituals, rhythm and blues songs, personal narratives, sermons, folktales, and so forth as pertinent to gaining a proper theological understanding of African American life and culture. In addition to calling attention to the neglect of African American culture in academic theology, black theologians attempt to show that the black experience is a unique and superior perspective from which to do theology. Cone's perspective realism of Christianity is an example of this tendency to revere blackness as a superior perspective, according to Jones.[14]

James Cone's liberation theology is not merely one Christian theology among many other plausible Christian theologies. He says, "Any interpretation of the gospel in any historical period that fails to see Jesus as the Liberator of the oppressed is heretical."[15] He says this because the norm of black theology, for him, is: "If the doctrine is compatible with or enhances the drive for black freedom, then it is the gospel of Jesus Christ. If the doctrine is against or indifferent to the essence of blackness as expressed in Black Power, then it is the work of Antichrist." Only those theologies compatible with Cone's are regarded by him as authentic expressions of Christianity. The black focus of Cone's perspective is presented as both identical to and expressive

---

14. Ibid., 514.
15. Cone, *God of the Oppressed*, 37.

of the essence of Christianity. His views on blackness ultimately determine which beliefs, doctrines, practices, and intellectual sources are worthy of incorporation into his system of theology.

The second stage in a developing academic discipline is the critical expansion phase. Here, the pioneer and earliest works in the field are used to define and justify the positions of those persons seeking entrance into the still new academic field. In place of white theologies, the earliest black theologies are used as a foil for theological newcomers to define, legitimate, and distinguish themselves in the relatively new field. According to Jones, the critical expansion phase signals a shift in interest away from justifying black theology before a largely white academic audience to the goal of validating a particular range of black theological opinion. This shift of interest is accompanied by conversations among black theologians on issues of methodology concerning the appropriate use of models, frameworks, sources, hermeneutical principles, and so forth.

J. Deotis Roberts is a helpful illustration of the critical expansion phase.[16] Roberts enters the field of black theology not by attacking white theology but rather by criticizing the black theologies of James Cone and Albert Cleage. Roberts argues that Cone and Cleage do not present black theologies that are authentically Christian because each fails to deal adequately with the theme of reconciliation. According to Roberts, Cleage neither deals realistically with sin nor expresses any optimism in God's grace to enable humans, black and white, to overcome sin. He understands Cleage to be saying:

> Sin is social or collective, but not personal. Love is to be operative only between soul brothers and sisters. It is the principle of unity and fellowship within the black nation, but does not enfold the white person.[17]

To Roberts, Cleage seems to have given up on reconciliation because he does not believe that whites can cease from the sins of oppression. Roberts is critical of what he sees as Cone's use of Christian language to legitimate the ideology of the black power movement and failure to interpret the whole gospel. He says emphatically, "A Chris-

---

16. Jones, "Toward an Interim Assessment of Black Theology," 515.
17. Roberts, *Liberation and Reconciliation,* revised ed., 25.

tian theologian is not an interpreter of the religion of Black Power."[18] For Roberts, the full gospel is not restricted solely to liberation. In his opinion, the emphasis of Christianity is not on social conflict but on the creation of a new humanity through the process of redemption of both oppressed and oppressors by means of liberation and their reconciliation into a new mode of relationship.[19] Thus, in presenting a black theology that is inclusive of reconciliation, Roberts stakes out a position for himself in a determined opposition to Cone and Cleage, the first two writers in contemporary black theology.

In the third and final phase of disciplinary development identified by Jones, the personal and intuitive insights of black theologians found in the first and second phases are replaced by an identification of and investigation into the essential elements and basic problems of black theology. The writing of black theologians in the second phase are highly personal and subjective in contrast to the third stage, which purports to be more objective. Jones's own work may be viewed as an initiation or a piece on the cutting edge of this third phase. As Jones argues, in the third phase of disciplinary development, black theologians must make explicit the ontological, anthropological, and ethical categories that presuppose the liberation theologies forged and constituting the traditions of expression in phases one and two. Only then will black theology have broken free from the subjective, confessional contexts that gave it birth.

Even prior to the developmental tasks of legitimation, critical expansion, and systematic construction, William R. Jones sees another task. He calls this task "gnosiological conversion."[20] He defines gnosiological conversion as "the liberation of the black mind from the destructive ideas and submissive attitudes that inhibit any movement toward authentic freedom."[21] In Jones's estimation, gnosiological conversion involves nothing less than a fundamental restructuring of oppressed blacks' present worldview and lifestyles. Henry Young similarly contends that the achievement of liberation requires a fundamental change in worldviews, especially modern notions of majority-minority rela-

---

18. Ibid., 5.
19. Ibid., 17.
20. Jones, *Is God a White Racist?* 67.
21. Ibid.

tions.[22] Cornel West concurs with both Jones and Young. West says that the black philosopher is the "one who brings the most subtle and sophisticated analytical tools to bear to explain and illuminate how structures of domination and effects of individual choices in language and in nondiscursive institutions operate."[23] He goes on to say that the central task of the black philosopher "is to stimulate, hasten, and enable alternative perceptions and practices by dislodging prevailing discourses and powers."[24]

Jones contends that gnosiological conversion is a complex task that is guided by at least three objectives.[25] First, the ideas and concepts that undergird oppression must be clearly isolated for study and criticism. Second, the related and supporting ideas, beliefs, myths, and so forth that serve to justify the oppression must be identified. Third, persuasive argumentation must be made for inciting persons to action that will result in the removal of the oppression and its supporting cast of ideas and system of justification.

Jones's conviction is that "the oppressed, in part, are oppressed precisely because they buy, or are indoctrinated to accept, a set of beliefs that negate those attitudes and actions necessary for liberation."[26] The task of the black philosopher is to convert African Americans, that is, to make them believers in the liberating quality of various systems of thought. Henry Young summarizes the tasks of the theologian as the interpretation of "the content of the Christian faith in the clearest and most intelligible manner possible."[27] This aim to make Christian faith intelligible is compatible with the goal of liberating the black mind. For Young, clarity of thought is crucial to freeing persons from false, nonliberating beliefs.

## CONTENT

For the Black Philosophical School, like the Black Hermeneutical School, liberation is the content of black theology, albeit with some

---

22. Henry J. Young, *Hope in Process: A Theology of Social Pluralism* (Minneapolis: Fortress Press, 1990), xvi.
23. West, *Keeping Faith,* 104–5.
24. Ibid., 83.
25. Jones, *Is God a White Racist?* 67–68.
26. Ibid., 41.
27. Young, *Hope in Process,* 76.

notable alterations. In the Black Hermeneutical School, liberation is defined using the Bible and black story. In the Black Philosophical School, liberation is not limited to the Bible or black story. Conceptions of liberation by thinkers in the Black Philosophical School, though, are not necessarily antithetical to conceptions of liberation espoused by thinkers in the Black Hermeneutical School who adhere closely to the Bible or black story. In the Black Philosophical School, liberation is defined using social and political philosophies that may or may not be compatible, at all points, with the Bible or black story. William R. Jones contends that liberation is contextual. For example, he believes that nonviolent social change aimed at racial integration can work and is to be desired, only if a specific set of favorable conditions obtain.[28] So, for Jones, the meaning of liberation as well as the means for achieving it are determined by the unique historical situation of an oppressed population. Without appeals to the Bible or black story, Anthony Pinn asserts that liberation is a vision of life leading to great opportunities for individual fulfillment and a better sense and appreciation of human worth.[29]

Alice Walker says that blacks and whites are the same basically. Both are human, but blacks tend to focus more on liberation. Why? She suspects that she and other black writers are heirs to a literary tradition based on slave narratives that are characterized by struggle to free body and soul from social ills more the making of whites than of themselves.[30] She defines this struggle as a quest for relationship in a life-affirming harmony. Humans are connected to every single thing on the earth. Her belief is that "only justice to every living thing (and everything is alive) will save humankind."[31] The salvation of humanity and liberation of the oppressed is tied to ecology, a respect for life, nature, and care of the environment.

For Walker, black liberation most likely means integration of the sort espoused by Martin Luther King Jr. She idolizes King and his wife Coretta. They, especially Martin, embody a particular philosophy

---

28. William R. Jones, "Liberation Strategies in Black Theology: mao, Martin, or Malcolm?" *Chicago Theological Seminary Register* 73 (winter 1983): 42.

29. Pinn, *Why Lord?* 13.

30. Alice Walker, *In Search of Our Mothers' Gardens* (San Diego: Harcourt Brace Jovanovich, 1983), 5.

31. Ibid., 342.

of race relations and theory of social change.[32] She celebrates Martin's early noneconomic liberalism, which focuses on the dignity, worth, and rights of the individual without calling into question the injustices endemic to American capitalism. King's philosophy and social activism gave birth, within her, to a sense of pride, a desire to learn and become her best.[33] She chose to engage herself in professional writing, which — while not bearing the same risks of physical danger faced by Martin and others — is still a courageous act for blacks denied this vocation. Black liberation is not only social, but also personal, according to Walker.

Being influenced by Marxist thought, Cornel West defines liberation within the context of overcoming capitalism and the myriad of social ills accompanied by it. He considers capitalism to be an antidemocratic mode of socioeconomic organization[34] that excludes from the enjoyment of the wealth and goods and services produced in a society those persons whose labor and suppression are essential to maintaining this system of production. Capitalism further results in the creation of "self-images and self-identities, values and sensibilities, institutions and associations, ways of life" that oppress individuals and groups of people, diminishing the quality of their lives by relegating them to poverty, disease, despair, and a lack of freedom and self-esteem.[35] According to West, capitalism results in four kinds of oppression: imperialism, classism, racism, and sexism.[36]

Henry Young defines liberation as cultural pluralism based upon Alfred North Whitehead's idea of organic pluralism — that is, how living or actual entities are related. Appropriating the insights of Whitehead's process metaphysics, Young contends that each social group must be actualized. He says:

> For social groups to achieve self-fulfillment, each has to possess a certain degree of power and independence. Without a sense of self-worth, self-identity, and self-determination, which is the basis of independence, no social group can attain fulfillment. This is to say, each social group should maintain its own unique cul-

---

32. Ibid., 124, 142–56.
33. Ibid., 125.
34. West, *Prophesy Deliverance!* 122.
35. Ibid., 123.
36. Ibid.

tural features through aesthetics, language, customs, mores, art forms, and history.[37]

This quest for self-fulfillment is not aimed at the separation of ethnic and social groups for the purpose of conflict. Instead, the goal of group self-determination, within the process worldview as Young understands it, is for each group "to co-exist peacefully alongside other social groups."[38]

## SOURCES

For the liberation of the black mind, Henry Young recommends process metaphysics, Cornel West pragmatism, and William R. Jones and Anthony Pinn humanism. Young contends that the organic pluralism which Alfred North Whitehead espoused serves as a better basis than traditional Newtonian metaphysics for constructing a vision of social pluralism that can elide social ills such as racism, sexism, classism, provincialism, ethnocentrism, and imperialism.[39] As Young sees it, on the one hand, Newtonian metaphysics is a mechanistic view of nature with fixed, static relations between entities (i.e., anything that exists), which are perceived in hierarchical arrangement. According to him, this mechanistic view of nature has reinforced the exploitation and depersonalization of minority groups in Western societies. In Newtonian thought, "nature [is] believed to be soundless, scentless, colorless, and meaningless."[40] Young points out that "just as it was necessary to denigrate nature as meaningless in order to coerce and degrade it, so it was necessary to associate blackness with degradation and inferiority in order to justify slavery."[41] "Slave masters in America taught the slaves that the apparent contradictions in life were forever binding and final. Their plight was fixed, finished, unchanging, and inescapable."[42] On the other hand, Whiteheadean metaphysics is a descriptive phenomenology of experience that views entities as being in a state of flux and therefore as not permanently occupying any fixed relations, including

---

37. Young, *Hope in Process,* 57–58.
38. Ibid., 58.
39. Ibid., xvi.
40. Ibid., 23.
41. Ibid., 24.
42. Ibid., 30.

hierarchical ones. According to Young, process metaphysics is "true to life" in that it permits acknowledgment of the occurrence and desirability of change and becoming in human civilization.[43] Whitehead's metaphysical perspective supports black liberation in the sense that present relations between blacks and whites, like any other relations, are in no way permanent. In the Whiteheadean view of the world, liberation is quite possible and achievable.

Cornel West views his reexamination and selective interpretation of American pragmatism as a "first step toward fundamental change and transformation in America and the world."[44] He calls his appropriation of American pragmatism "prophetic criticism."[45] West also uses the phrase "prophetic thought" to refer to his broad program of pragmatism.[46] He asserts that this intellectual tradition demystifies the complex dynamics of massive social structures and institutions, thereby generating "options and alternatives for transforming praxis."[47] West's perspective is similar to Young's perspective with respect to each one's emphasis on the necessity of grasping intellectually possibilities for achieving and maximizing freedom.[48]

For Cornel West, "pragmatism has to do with trying to conceive of knowledge, reality, and truth in such a way that it promotes the flowering and flourishing of individuality under conditions of democracy."[49] Pragmatism is a philosophical movement that has as its goal the creation and maintenance of democracy.[50] As he understands pragmatism, its view of knowledge, reality, and truth is captured in three slogans: voluntarism, fallibilism, and experimentalism.[51] Voluntarism is the emphasis of pragmatists on human will, human power, and human action in the resolution of economic, social, political, or intellectual problems. Fallibilism means that every claim is open to criticism and revision. Experimentalism is the view that experience and the knowledge gained

---

43. Ibid., 42.

44. Cornel West, *The American Evasion of Philosophy: A Genealogy of Pragmatism* (Madison: University of Wisconsin Press, 1989), 8.

45. West, *Keeping Faith*, 104.

46. Cornel West, *Prophetic Thought in Postmodern Times*, vol. 1, *Beyond Eurocentrism and Multiculturalism* (Monroe, Maine: Common Courage Press, 1993), 3.

47. Ibid., 23–24.

48. Young, *Hope in Process,* 125–26.

49. West, *Prophetic Thought,* 32.

50. Ibid., 43.

51. Ibid., 37, 43.

from it are governed by a process of trial and error. In addition, competing ideas and courses of action are adjudicated by determinations on which ones work best in experience.

West's choice of pragmatism is rooted in his acknowledgment of prophetic Christian thought as a source for theological reflection. According to him, prophetic Christian thought is characterized by the belief that "every individual regardless of class, country, caste, race, or sex should have the opportunity to fulfill his or her potentialities."[52] This radical egalitarian ideal emphasizes "the self-realization of individuality within community."[53] From Christianity West finds and, as a professing Christian, holds firmly to the belief that humans are equal and should live within a community allowing for each individual's realization. He says:

> democracy itself is still a means. And it is a means for the flowering of individuality. Why do I see it this way? Because I stand fundamentally on the profoundly Christian notion that we are equal in the eyes of God.[54]

Democracy is the form of social organization and government most compatible with the principle of Christian egalitarianism, according to West.[55] Since the desired end of pragmatism is democracy, as mentioned above, West reasonably chooses pragmatism as a source in his theological reflection.

William R. Jones and Anthony Pinn contend that humanism is, and must be regarded as, a source in academic black theology. According to both, black theologians deal selectively with African American religion, choosing only the theistic tradition in African American thought. However, African American religious experience is heterogeneous — that is, made up of various modes of expression. According to Jones, humanism is a philosophical perspective that rivals Christian theism and points out its inadequacies in the explanation of black suffering and development of viable theologies of liberation.[56] He contends that there is documentary evidence that shows that humanism's origin

---

52. West, *Prophesy Deliverance!* 15.
53. Ibid.
54. West, *Prophetic Thought,* 63.
55. West, *Prophesy Deliverance!* 18.
56. Jones, "Religious Humanism," 169–70, 173, 179.

is simultaneous to the evangelism of African slaves. For example, in secular or nonreligious songs, slaves ridiculed their fellow slaves for worshipping God and anticipating compensation in another world for their present deprivation.[57] In addition to these songs, the testimony of evangelists to slave communities, such as Daniel Alexander Payne and Charles C. Jones, reveals slaves' open contempt and rejection of Christianity.[58] Payne encountered slaves who rejected Christianity altogether because of the brutality of their Christian masters. Charles Jones observed various belief patterns among the slaves, including humanistic thought.

Like William R. Jones, Anthony Pinn contends that African American religious experience is heterogeneous. As such, the study and theological interpretation of African American religion must include humanism. As Pinn sees it, humanism gives persons some sense of orientation and place within the world. He says, "Humanism is a religious system because it provides a framework that guides human conduct and connects this conduct to the larger reality of Black community."[59] In addition to humanism, Pinn asserts that other religious systems are worthy of consideration in the study and theological interpretation of African American religion. In a work entitled *Varieties of African American Religious Experience* (1998), he examines four belief systems among African Americans: Voodoo, Santeria and Orisha devotion, Islam, and humanism. In contrast to black Christian denominational histories that focus on organizational developments and doctrines, Pinn's work highlights the popular practices and subtle influences of these belief systems.

While Jones and Pinn both commend humanism in the construction of black liberationist thought, each pursues a separate path of thought leading to different conclusions. Jones concludes that black theology can never be anything more than an extended theodicy that must reconcile the empirical reality of black suffering with beliefs about God's benevolence and power.[60] If theodicy is likened to an equation having a balanced harmony between a particular model of theism and a particular conception of suffering, then one can report that Jones focuses

57. Ibid., 171.
58. Ibid., 170, 172.
59. Pinn, *Why Lord?* 19.
60. Jones, *Is God a White Racist?* xx–xxi.

his criticism on the theistic side of the equation. Jones contends that the most profitable course for a critical review of black theology is the investigation of the prevailing image of God rather than a probe into the suffering of the oppressed. A reflection on suffering yields only a more intimate sense of the oppressed's pain and does not seriously affect an assessment of the theodicy in question.[61] Thus, Jones directs his sharpest criticism toward the prevailing model of God in black theology, black liberation theism.

In Jones's opinion, black liberation theism contains "a fatal residue of the oppressor's world view."[62] In all of its particular formulations, black liberation theism is based on traditional Western-biblical theism, which inhibits any movement toward authentic liberation. According to Jones, traditional Western theism makes holiness and justice intrinsic properties of God.[63] The perfect goodness of God is a given, a property not accessible to questioning or subject to empirical verification. In the absence of empirical verification, oppressed African Americans who buy into the traditional view of God settle for an eschatological verification of God's goodness despite their past and present experiences, which suggest they ought to believe otherwise. The racist quality of God remains hidden. That is, the beliefs about God that are antithetical to the liberation of African Americans are not subject to critical review. As Jones points out, "a racist God is theologically impossible where God's universal benevolence is presupposed."[64] When holiness and justice are intrinsic properties of God, oppressed persons who believe in God can never see God as an instrument of oppression opposed to the improvement of their quality of life.

Anthony Pinn rejects the category of theodicy because it entails a commitment to redemptive suffering. According to Pinn, the notion of redemptive suffering inhibits liberation and therefore must be abandoned.[65] The ill consequence of the concept of redemptive suffering is that African Americans' suffering is justified and tolerated by appeals to divine plans that God has for the betterment of American society.[66]

---

61. Ibid., 9, 56.
62. Ibid., 77.
63. Ibid., 7.
64. Ibid., 33.
65. Pinn, *Why Lord?* 17–18.
66. Ibid., 16, 89.

He says that these plans are usually shrouded in mystery — that is to say, they are always incapable of empirical verification.[67]

## THE BLACK EXPERIENCE

As with the Black Hermeneutical School, the black experience, in all of its multiple dimensions, is a source for theological reflection in the Black Philosophical School. For Cornel West, African American experience is a source for constructive thought. The study of black life and thought is a necessity for the pragmatist philosopher and Christian theologian intent on achieving democracy. Speaking in reference to the plight of oppressed African Americans, West writes, "It seems to me any serious reflections about the possibilities for expanding freedom and democracy in the USA have to do with coming to terms with this hard case."[68] His understanding is that prophetic thought is not abstract but deeply contextual and explicit about the kinds of actions persons must take in order to achieve a state of genuine democracy in American society.

For Alice Walker, African American women's experience is an important source for her writing. As a womanist, she appreciates and prefers women's culture. By women's culture, she means "Black women's particular forms of creativity in language, writing, relationships, religious and political understandings, moral values, and articles of beauty that Black women have created for everyday use from flower gardens to quilts to blues and literature."[69] A womanist loves women. But these are not her only loves. She also loves men, music, dance, the moon, the spirit, and more. According to Walker, the writer must embrace everything in order to reach the truth and thus present an accurate image of humanity.[70]

Though highly significant for theological reflection, the black experience is not considered to be normative. As I mentioned earlier in my discussion on the Black Philosophical School, William R. Jones says that race is not the organizing principle of black philosophy. He says that his own experience — that is, his life and involvement in the black church — puts before him issues like the need to make sense of

---

67. Ibid., 16.
68. West, *Prophetic Thought,* 59.
69. Karen Baker-Fletcher and Garth Kasimu Baker-Fletcher, *My Sister, My Brother,* 3.
70. Walker, *In Search of Our Mothers' Gardens,* 137.

and eradicate black people's suffering. However, he does not feel compelled to accept theological explanations of black suffering formulated by the black church.[71]

## OTHER SOURCES

In addition to the black experience, other sources in the Black Philosophical School include revelation, scripture, tradition, church history and culture, and reason. Henry Young modifies these sources, making them more suitable to the logical constraints of process metaphysics. With respect to revelation, black theology must focus on the authentic revelatory experiences of African Americans. However, he contends that these revelatory experiences should not be regarded as exclusive, i.e., fully representative of God's nature.[72] God's self-disclosure cannot be assigned exclusively to any particular group or religious tradition.[73]

Young says that scripture is significant not because of some feature of the texts regarded as sacred by Christians, but because of the convictions that Christians hold about it. Scripture is believed to be a record of revelatory experiences that are foundational to Christianity. Because African Americans use the Bible as a historical reference point for anchoring their respective faith communities, exegesis and hermeneutics become useful tools in black theology, according to Young.[74] He defines the concept of tradition broadly to encompass the variety of cultural forms peculiar to a particular faith community. These cultural forms would include many of the same sources of the black experience mentioned in the Black Hermeneutical School such as sermons, prayers, religious and secular songs (e.g., spirituals and the blues), folktales, personal narratives, black literature (e.g., fiction and poetry), and worship style. To the list of cultural forms constituting tradition, Cornel West would add modes of praxis, that is, theoretical frameworks that structure African Americans' thought and action.

Cornel West contends that there are four traditions of African American responses to racism. They are exceptionalism (i.e., pride, self-help, heroism), assimilationism (i.e., self-hate, shame, fear), marginalism (i.e., creativity or conformity, revolt or withdrawal), and humanism

---

71. Jones, *Is God a White Racist?* xiv–xv.
72. Young, *Hope in Process*, 96–97.
73. Ibid., 89.
74. Ibid., 97.

(i.e., realism, honest confrontation with past, pragmatic change).[75] West also contends that two principle traditions are vehicles for the structure and expression of black intellectualism. They are the black Christian tradition of preaching and the musical tradition of performance.[76] I described the black preaching tradition in chapter 1. West's choice mode of expression is preaching and preferred tradition of response to racism is humanism.

As a source for theology, reason sets apart the Black Philosophical School from other schools. Henry Young defines reason as knowledge or intelligence in the service of improving the quality of human life.[77] Common to Henry Young, Cornel West, Anthony Pinn, and William R. Jones is reason in the form of philosophical traditions. As we have seen, humanism is the principal philosophical tradition utilized in the theological reflection of Jones and Pinn. Young utilizes process metaphysics. West's thinking is informed greatly by pragmatism. His commitment to pragmatism influences his selection and use of Antonio Gramsci's neo-Marxism as a suitable form of social analysis that critiques American and Western civilization and advances black liberation.[78]

Cornel West believes that Marxist social analysis describes the situation of oppression and recommends actions for its eradication. As he sees it, the limitations and shortcomings of most of academic black theology are:

1. Its lack of a systematic social analysis, which has prevented black theologians from coming to terms with the relationships between racism, sexism, class exploitation, and imperialist oppression

2. Its lack of a social vision, political program, and concrete praxis, which defines and facilitates socioeconomic and political liberation

3. Its tendency to downplay existential issues such as death, disease, dread, despair, and disappointment, which are related to, yet not identical with, suffering caused by oppressive structures[79]

75. West, *Prophesy Deliverance!* 69–91.
76. West, *Keeping Faith*, 72–73.
77. Young, *Hope in Process*, 108.
78. West, *Keeping Faith*, 204–5.
79. West, *Prophesy Deliverance!* 106.

West recommends Marxism as the system of thought that will enable black theology to overcome these limitations and shortcomings. In his opinion, Marxism is anticapitalist, anti-imperialist, antiracist, and anti-sexist and possesses a democratic socialist vision of society.[80] He thinks that Antonio Gramsci's version of Marxism is the most progressive form of Marxism and provides an explicit program of liberation that is compatible with the aims of black theology.[81] Gramsci views culture not only in the traditional Marxist terms of power and economic and class struggle but also in terms of the ideas, behaviors, sensibilities, and so forth that support and sanction an existing social order. He corre-lates liberation of the mind with economic and political liberation. As I discussed earlier, gnosiological conversion, the liberation of the black mind, is a major concern of thinkers in the Black Philosophical School. For West, this task of liberating the black mind provides an opening for scholars to enter the field of social activism or to demonstrate the relevance of their work to economic and political liberation.

## NORM

The norm of the Black Philosophical School is to be found in human-istic conceptions of Christian faith. That is to say, thinkers in the Black Philosophical School ground academic black theology in humanism. These humanistic conceptions of Christian faith are both positive and negative. William R. Jones, Henry Young and Cornel West in various ways modify or affirm Christian faith but Anthony Pinn denies its au-thority altogether in academic scholarship and black liberation. Alice Walker's brand of humanism causes her to vacillate between atheism and agnosticism.

### DEFINING HUMANISM

William R. Jones and Anthony Pinn define humanism in the follow-ing manner. According to Jones, two affirmations lie at the center of humanism: (1) freedom is the essence of human being and (2) human choice is logically prior to the authority of faith, reason, science,

---

80. Ibid.
81. Ibid., 118–19.

method, and so forth.[82] To Jones's assertion Pinn adds the proposition that black humanism is expressed in weak and strong versions. He says that weak humanism

> entails an increased sense of self and one's place in the human family. This position does not call God's existence into question. Anxiety arises, for weak humanists, when reflecting upon the realm of God's activity in the world; not over the very existence of God. It sees enough evidence of divine activity to leave unchallenged God's place in the universe. But there is not enough evidence for the weak humanist to confidently proclaim divine activity as the sole factor in historical happenings. World affairs seem the result of joint effort — God and humanity. Furthermore, God's existence is not questioned because weak humanism seeks — in response to oppressive conditions — the increased status of Black humanity relative to that of white humanity. It is a matter of humans seeking parity with other humans. The goal is to prevent the oppressed from underestimating their humanity and oppressors from overstating their humanity.[83]

In sum, weak humanism seeks the liberation of oppressed African Americans without calling into question or denying the existence of God. It emphasizes a greater sense of self, one's place in the human family, and the powers in one's self put there by God. About strong humanism, he says:

> Relatively sustained and oppressive world conditions bring into question the presence of any Being outside of the human realm. The record of temporal developments does not bear the noticeable imprint of any One beyond humanity; moments of achievement are far too serendipitous to promote a teleological perspective and conviction that there is cosmic companionship. Consequently, humanity has no one to turn to for assistance. Furthermore, oppressive circumstances do not point to a level of activity beyond the scope of human capability. That is, moral evil in the world is easily understood as the result of misguided "will

---

82. William R. Jones, "Functional Ultimacy as Authority in Religious Humanism," *Religious Humanism* 12 (winter 1978): 29–31.

83. Pinn, *Why Lord?* 141.

to power" and nothing more. As a result, strong humanism also
denies the existence of an evil God who is responsible for human
suffering. Hence, strong humanism seeks to combat oppression
through radical human commitment to life and corresponding
activity.[84]

In sum, strong humanism places human life in the hands of humans.
It denies the existence of God, be this God good or evil. Humans
are solely responsible for their actions and future. Strong humanism
does not view suffering as redemptive but only as a thing to be eradi-
cated. Pinn contends that this drive to overcome suffering is inspired
sufficiently by humans' hope of change; there is no need for God.[85]

According to Anthony Pinn's description of weak and strong humanism, by his own admission, he is a strong humanist. William R.
Jones, Alice Walker, Cornel West, and Henry Young are weak humanists. Pinn points out that Jones and West subscribe to weak
humanism.[86] However, he does not examine Walker's and Young's
works. But their works, I believe, may be classified under the head-
ing of weak humanism. Jones does not deny the existence of God.
He critiques the black liberation theism of the Black Hermeneutical
School and offers in place of it what he calls humanocentric theism.
He recognizes theodicy as the controlling category of black theology
and therefore acknowledges that God-talk or the affirmation of God's
existence is basic to what black theology is. He thinks that no black
theologian needs to give up belief in God.[87] If West adheres to what
he calls prophetic Christianity, which is characterized essentially by the
belief that all persons are equal in the sight of God, then he does affirm God's existence. Because process theism falls under what Jones
contends is the category of humanocentric theism — that is, Christian
theism that emphasizes human freedom and God's use of persuasive
power in human affairs — Young's use of process theology makes him
a weak humanist along with Jones and West. Walker affirms belief in
God as nature-centered spirit rather than a traditional Western notion
of deity.

---

84. Ibid.
85. Ibid., 157–58.
86. Ibid., 145.
87. Jones, *Is God a White Racist?* 172.

While Pinn considers himself to be a strong humanist, he contends that he is not alone. He says that strong humanism is found in African American oral traditions (i.e., folklore, the blues, hip-hop, and rap music) and the literature written by Richard Wright and Nella Larsen.[88] Pinn's distinction between strong and weak humanism should not be taken to mean that no significant differences exist between himself, Jones, Walker, West, and Young. He employs the distinction not to obliterate difference but rather to broaden the concept of humanism in black religious thought to include both positive and negative interpretations of Christian faith.

## JONES'S HUMANOCENTRIC THEISM

Through his critique of black liberation theism, William R. Jones develops his conception of humanocentric theism, which he seeks to make normative for academic black theology. He defines "black liberation theism" as the belief that God identifies with and is on the side of oppressed African Americans and will liberate them. He contends that the works of all leading black theologians, most of whom are in the Black Hermeneutical School, affirm that God is working for human liberation and that God is on the side of oppressed African Americans.[89] Propositions basic to black liberation theism may be elucidated as follows:

1. God exists and is omnipotent, omniscient, and perfectly good.

2. God identifies and is one with black people.

3. Black people experience a form of negative suffering properly referred to as oppression.

4. A perfectly good God, who is omniscient, omnipotent, and identifies with black people, will liberate them from oppression.

Proposition 2 can be understood to mean — in its most popular usage among black theologians — that God is black. This identification and solidarity with black people establishes the divine nature as black. Black liberation theologians differ over what constitutes God's

88. Pinn, *Why Lord?* 11, 117, 121–22, 148, 150.
89. Jones, *Is God a White Racist?* 75.

blackness. No black theologian seems to deny that some quality or property of blackness is present in God's nature. However, an enduring question among black theologians is "Is God's blackness a matter of skin pigmentation, shared values with African Americans, sensitivity to the plight of the oppressed, predisposition to love the oppressed, or partnership in the struggle for liberation?"

Proposition 3 presupposes that suffering is an inescapable aspect of human life. Jones argues that suffering is part and parcel to the human condition.[90] Also presupposed is the notion that suffering can manifest itself in several forms. Forms of suffering that are not redemptive, that is, those that do not lead to some greater good, are meaningless and are to be avoided or eliminated. According to Jones, suffering in a general sense is not problematic. Suffering becomes problematic when it takes on a negative quality. Some forms of suffering have positive value in that one's endurance of them makes possible the attainment of what one perceives to be his or her highest good.

For example, sore and aching muscles resulting from one's training for Olympic competition is not problematic. This type of suffering is unavoidable and may contribute to one's achievement of the reward of a gold, silver, or bronze medal. Sore and aching muscles because of one's being forced to labor without pay or fair compensation is a form of suffering that is problematic. The endurance or acceptance of this negative form of suffering is not in one's best interest. Conceivably under a different economic system, one's toil would contribute more toward one's fulfillment than if present working conditions were to remain the same. Oppression is a form of suffering that does not lead or contribute to a greater good for African Americans.

Closely related to and following from proposition 3 is proposition 4. Proposition 4 makes liberation a matter of freedom from the negative suffering unique to oppression rather than a blissful deliverance from all suffering. Liberation is not deliverance from all suffering but only from that suffering which lies at the core of oppression.[91]

Jones maintains that propositions 2 and 4 are inconsistent with proposition 3. Jones argues that

90. Ibid., xviii.
91. Ibid., 28.

If God were black, then God would liberate black people from oppression.

God has not liberated, is not liberating, or will not liberate black people from oppression.

Then, God is not black.

Therefore, God is a white racist.

Jones states that insufficient evidence is available to warrant any belief that God is in solidarity with black people and will liberate them. The continued misery of African Americans is indispensable evidence that God is not black.[92] If God were black, then God would be a fellow sufferer who is both knowledgeable of and desirous of relief from the pain of oppression. As a fellow sufferer with ultimate power, God should liberate African Americans. The fact of white racism, its continuing presence, is a contradiction to the belief in an all-powerful and perfectly good "black God." According to Jones, no evidence leads to or supports belief in a black God.[93]

In William R. Jones's opinion, citing biblical motifs of God's supposed acts of liberation and the verification of black liberation theism in the postulation of a future eschaton does not constitute sufficient evidence.[94] On the one hand, Jones argues that biblical motifs are not direct acts of divine liberation in the history of African Americans. A legitimately held belief in black liberation theism requires what he calls a "liberation-exaltation event." That is to say, belief in black liberation theism would be justified if a definitive event in African American history had clearly demonstrated that God favors African Americans and is working to liberate them.[95] However, according to Jones, even if the identification of some event (or events) were made, no useful results would follow. An empirical event may be integrated into opposing views. The African American condition may be, and often is, seen differently by black theologians as either the liberating handiwork of God or an ever spreading genocide.[96]

---

92. Ibid., 27.
93. Ibid., 36.
94. Ibid., 18–20, 114–16.
95. Ibid., 114, 116.
96. Ibid., 8–9.

For proof of the split among black theologians, Jones points to James Cone, Joseph Washington, and J. Deotis Roberts's claims to have discovered signs of God's liberating activity among African Americans while Samuel Yette claims to see only genocide occurring among African Americans. On the other hand, Jones argues that eschatological verification does not add to our certainty but instead begs the question of why God is delaying liberation.[97] Is God able but not willing or is God willing but not able to liberate black people? Jones goes further to say that black theologians lack any historical precedent in choosing to verify God's goodness using eschatology. He emphasizes that African concepts of time and history do not attribute any normative status to the future.[98] African concepts of time emphasize the past. Jones insists that if indigenous African sources are given due consideration in black theology, black theologians must abandon any future orientation with respect to explaining God's nature and actions.

## THE PROBLEM OF DIVINE RACISM

In stating that God is a white racist, William R. Jones means that God does not identify with and is hostile or unsympathetic toward black people. God can be more easily aligned with whites than blacks. God's delay or inaction serves only to continue the advantage of whites over blacks. This hostility, lack of sympathy, or indifference on the part of God is what Jones calls "divine racism."

Jones contends that theodicies based on black liberation theism cannot refute the charge of divine racism, whether true or false, after it is raised. None of the black theologians whom he examines have developed a system of interpretation that adequately deals with this challenge to the goodness of God. Jones points out that this challenge is serious. The insinuation that God either sides with, is hostile to, or ambivalent toward any group of people is a serious indictment against God's capacity to love and care for all humankind.

Jones suggests that the problem of divine racism emerges not only in black liberation theism but in any theistic framework that puts God in solidarity with an oppressed community or class of people.[99] Any oppressed group that claims that God sides with it must sooner or

---

97. Ibid., 12.
98. Ibid., 14.
99. Ibid., xvii, 23.

later deal with evidence that points to the contrary. Any oppressed group that claims that God sides with it must deal with those experiences or events that raise doubts concerning God's solidarity with the oppressed.

As Jones says, if the principal task of the black theologian is to liberate the black mind from the destructive ideas and submissive attitudes that checkmate any movement toward authentic emancipation, then all the leading black theologians fail in this task by virtue of their adherence to some variation of black liberation theism. In Jones's opinion, black liberation theism contains "a fatal residue of the [white] oppressors' world view."[100] Black theologians are blind to the incongruence of their model of theism to the oppressed condition of the people whom they seek to liberate. Black liberation theism falls short of the freedom of thought possible when the voices of black protest are allowed, as Jones contends they ought, to extend all the way to a critical questioning and abandonment of the traditional Judeo-Christian view of God and search for an alternative.[101]

In view of what William R. Jones sees as the actual limited potential of black liberation theism to serve as a means of authentic emancipation, he claims that "humanocentric theism" is its only rational alternative. Humanocentric theism emphasizes the functional ultimacy of free human agents in history. Humans are held responsible for the existence of moral evil. God is not charged with indifference, hostility, or partiality toward any group of people. Humanocentric theism, the last point on the theistic spectrum before adopting a position of complete humanism, is the only legitimate option for someone convinced of the inadequacies of black liberation theism but yet committed to explaining the suffering of African Americans using a theistic framework.

## HUMAN FREEDOM

In contrast to the theologians who develop theologies of liberation based on the activity, purpose, revelation, or will of God, William R. Jones prefers to achieve the goal of formulating a liberating theology through emphasis on what he labels the "functional ultimacy" of

---

100. Ibid., 77.
101. Ibid., 25.

humans.[102] By functional ultimacy, Jones means the decisive role of humans in the interpretation and valuation of their existence. Jones contends that humanity, not God, is "the final interpreter, valuator, or arbiter in the arena of truth and values."[103] In other words, human freedom is the actual foundation for ultimate norms and determinations of truth and values.

Jones's views on the determinative role of human freedom do not nullify theism. He merely points out that whereas God may be thought of as the creator of reality, humans are its interpreters. According to Jones, freedom — the capacity to think, feel, choose, and interpret, citing oneself as the sufficient cause or determining factor — is the essence of human nature.[104] Jones says that this authority of humans to act as interpreters of their experience is analogous to the functioning of the U.S. Supreme Court. The Court exercises the power to interpret the nation's Constitution. While interpreting and altering public understanding concerning the Constitution, the Court does not create this Constitution. The Court interprets a document that it did not originate. Similarly, humans interpret and shape a reality that they did not originate or call into existence.

William R. Jones's proof or support of functional ultimacy is "the multievidentiality of events and propositions."[105] Jones points out that the same event may have not only several but also opposing interpretations of equal validity. Persons may describe events differently. Based upon their personal witness and available knowledge, each person may be correct. In addition, the truth or falsity of propositions is not always self-evident nor demonstrable. That which humans assert as true is never immune to questioning or revision. Jones contends that humans live in a situation of "objective uncertainty." For Jones, the humanistic view of life corresponds to this condition in human existence. Humanism acknowledges the radical freedom of humans, their ultimacy of choice, and the fragility of their most certain knowledge. In order to live, to exist with any sense of fulfillment, humans must make choices not only about various aspects of reality but also about God as the highest reality.

---

102. Ibid., 68.
103. Jones, "Functional Ultimacy," 29.
104. Ibid.
105. Ibid., 30.

## HUMANOCENTRIC THEISM

Humanocentric theism affirms and exalts the radical freedom of humans to the degree they become a codetermining power with God.[106] Under the humanocentric model of theism, humans act to control those areas of human life traditionally restricted to God, such as war, famine, environmental hazards, reproduction, and so on. The exercise of this radical freedom is best understood as a consequence of God's having created humans as free agents. Human freedom does not compromise the status of God but rather conforms to God's will, ultimate plan, and purpose for human life.[107]

William R. Jones identifies and explains three essential tenets of humanocentric theism.[108] These core beliefs are not only basic to this model of theism but also serve to categorize any particular theism as humanocentric. Cornel West's and Henry Young's conceptions of Christian faith and Alice Walker's pantheistic nature spirituality adhere to these tenets of the humanocentric theism that Jones recognized.

The first essential tenet of humanocentric theism is a belief in humanity's codeterminacy power with God. This codetermining power is believed to be intrinsic to human nature by virtue of God's creation of humans as free agents. Along with this freedom to act comes the human share of responsibility for both the evil and the good in life.

A second belief characterizing humanocentric theism is the belief that human activity, choice, and freedom are necessary conditions for the attainment of humanity's highest good. In other words, humans cannot experience the good without the exercise of their freedom, choice, and the exertion of effort. The good is not possible unless humans act. The good will not fall upon them by sheer luck.

A third tenet of humanocentric theism is the belief that the choices and actions of humanity limit God's sovereignty. Further, this limitation is believed to be self-imposed. Because God respects human freedom, God's exercise of power is through persuasion rather than coercion. God arouses, suggests, influences, and sustains human action but never controls or demands that human action take any particular

---

106. William R. Jones, "Is Faith in God Necessary for a Just Society? Insights from Liberation Theology," in *The Search for Faith and Justice*, ed. Gene G. James (New York: Paragon, 1987), 92.
107. Jones, *Is God a White Racist?* 187.
108. Ibid., 188–94.

course. God may still be thought of as being supremely powerful, albeit with the stipulation that coercion is not consistent with God's nature or purpose.

The propositions that are basic to Jones's outline and argument for humanocentric theism are as follows:

> God exists and is omniscient, perfectly good, and supremely powerful.
>
> God created humans with the capacity to act as free agents.
>
> Black people experience a form of negative suffering called oppression.
>
> Humans, black and white, are responsible for suffering stemming from moral evils such as oppression and have the power(s) to eliminate suffering.
>
> Therefore, God is involved in history by way of God's exercise of persuasive power only because of God's will and decision to respect the freedom of human beings.

As Jones presents it, humanocentric theism emphasizes that history is open-ended. God persuades but cannot or does not force humans to act. History is the result of the interplay between free human agents. The elimination of oppression is therefore a task whose execution is left up to humans.

## CONSEQUENCES OF HUMANOCENTRIC THEISM

In discussing the strengths of humanocentric theism, William R. Jones points to four positive consequences that would follow from its adoption.[109] First, humanocentric theism provides for an accommodation of human freedom, a framework that is essential to liberation theology. A liberation theology that seeks to motivate an oppressed people to action must recognize them as centers of power and agents of transformation, which is precisely what humanocentric theism does, according to Jones.[110] Humanocentric theism instills within the oppressed the notion that they are not powerless or helpless. They are

---

109. Ibid., 194–97.
110. Jones, "Is Faith in God Necessary for a Just Society?" 93.

free to act, and their choices do matter in terms of affecting their predicament.

Second, humanocentric theism consistently refutes the charge of divine racism, removing God from the side of any group. If God does favor or elect any group, such preference is of limited consequence for human history. Human history is the result of the interplay of human agents as they respond to or reject divine persuasion. No group is predestined for success or doomed to failure.

Third, humanocentric theism makes people, both oppressed and nonoppressed, responsible for their life situations. Because history is not controlled by God in any domineering fashion, God is not responsible for any existing human life situations, good or bad. Human choice and action are decisive in the matter of liberation. Human action serves to either frustrate or promote justice.

Fourth, humanocentric theism is the best theistic response to modern secularism. Modern people believe less and less in God. Few persons trust God to perform miracles or intervene in history. The adoption of a theistic framework that emphasizes the determinative role of human freedom would be more palatable to the sensibilities of modern culture.

In spite of humanocentric theism's logical consistency and positive value, William R. Jones points out at least four grim consequences that humanocentric theism entails.[111] First, if black theologians shift from black liberation theism to humanocentric theism, they will have to abandon the belief in and talk of God's solidarity with oppressed African Americans. Second, and closely related to the first, is the consequence of abandoning talk about the inevitable liberation of the oppressed. If history is open-ended — the result of human choices (some of which may be a rejection of God's persuasion or suggestions for good) — then whether God guarantees the ultimate triumph of justice is questionable. Third, no specific historical events may be selected as God's handiwork or presence in history. Because of their multievidentiality, events that may be labeled as God's acts of persuasion are subject to opposing views. Compelling arguments could show that an event may, as well as may not, be an act of God. Fourth, God

---

111. Jones, *Is God a White Racist?* 201–2; idem, "Process Theology: Guardian of the Oppressor or Goad to the Oppressed — An Interim Assessment," *Process Studies* 18, no. 4 (winter 1989): 278–79.

could probably be an evil deity. Because of the multievidentiality of events, God's goodness is incapable of any objective certainty or empirical verification. Biblical motifs and eschatological verification do not result in adequate proof of God's goodness.

Though Jones claims that humanocentric theism is the only rational alternative to black liberation theism, he is skeptical of humanocentric theism's potential to serve as an instrument and inspiration for social justice. Jones finds unnerving the thought of God's absolute neutrality. Humanocentric theism implies that God is not on anyone's side, in which case God's intent or purpose for human history is unclear.[112] God may even be demonic or indifferent. The liberation of the oppressed is not inevitable, and whether African Americans' liberation is both a present and imminent possibility is uncertain. The abolition of racism is not seen as a real possibility. If liberation will ever happen, then its occurrence is contingent upon the unpredictable interplay between free human agents.

William R. Jones's honest thought is that theism, of any form, is not sufficient or necessary for the attainment of a just society.[113] The phenomena that characterize human life need not be interpreted as acts of God or as consistent or inconsistent with God's will and purpose. As Jones says repeatedly, events are multievidential, capable of several valid interpretations. Theism is not the only framework for interpreting human life.

For Jones, secular humanism is the most viable model for liberation. The only appeal of humanocentric theism is its theistic framework. No black theologian would be prepared to give up belief in God altogether. According to Jones, humanocentric theism is the last point on the theistic spectrum before one jumps to a position of complete humanism.[114] Humanocentric theism is as close as a theologian can move toward secular humanism.

In view of both the positive value and grim consequences of humanocentric theism as well as the pain of black suffering, William R. Jones contends that any viable theodicy must satisfy twelve requirements.[115] As I mentioned earlier, Anthony Pinn rejects the notion of

---

112. Jones, "Process Theology," 278.
113. Jones, "Is Faith in God Necessary for a Just Society?" 85.
114. Jones, *Is God a White Racist?* 172.
115. Ibid., 174–75.

theodicy as a central category for black theology. Nevertheless, for Jones:

1. God cannot be the ultimate blame for ethnic suffering.

2. The refutation of divine racism must be drawn from actual physical happenings in African American life.

3. The charge of divine racism cannot be reintroduced at another level or in another form.

4. The charge of divine racism should not lead to other insinuations of God's hostility or indifference, for example, toward women, whites, and other social groups.

5. The general framework must be monotheistic. Such a framework prohibits the creation of a demon to explain the presence of evil.

6. Ethnic suffering cannot be explained away as a deserved punishment.

7. The theodicy must not use eschatological verification as a way of determining whether God is indeed benevolent.

8. The liberation of African Americans must be both a present and future possibility before the eschaton, the end of time.

9. Oppression must be defined as a negative suffering that contributes nothing toward the enhancement of human life and which therefore ought to be eliminated.

10. Human action must be viewed as an essential and necessary ingredient for liberation.

11. The abolition of racism must be considered a real possibility.

12. Commonly accepted logical canons must be respected. The theodicy must be "internally consistent and systematically coherent."

## WEST'S PRAGMATISM

Cornel West's conception of Christian faith, the product of his blending humanism and pragmatism with prophetic Christian thought, is compatible with Jones's description of humanocentric theism. Concerning the African American humanist tradition, West says that its norms of individuality and democratic control of the political and productive processes are acceptable because they promote personal development, cultural growth, and human freedom. They foster the fulfillment of the potentialities and capacities of all individuals, encourage innovation and originality in Afro-American culture, and expand people's control over those institutions which deeply affect their lives.[116]

As mentioned earlier, for West, prophetic Christian thought is characterized essentially by belief in egalitarianism — a belief in self-realization within democratic community. He finds in African American humanism norms that are congenial to his preferred mode of expression in the prophetic tradition of Christianity. As I discussed earlier in the section on sources, for West, pragmatism (as expressed in the slogans of voluntarism, fallibilism, and experimentalism) extols the role of human will and agency in truth, knowledge, value, and social change. As a pragmatist, he sees the future as open, risk-ridden, and greatly influenced, if not determined, by humans rather than God.[117] His blending of prophetic Christian thought with humanism and pragmatism leads him

to the conception of a universe whose evolution is not finished, of a universe which is still, in [William] James's term, "in the making." In the process of becoming. Up to a certain point, still plastic. For pragmatism, "in the future" has ethical significance because human will, human thought and action, can make a difference in relation to human aims and purposes. There is moral substance in the fact that human will can make the future different and possibly better.[118]

### YOUNG'S PROCESS THOUGHT

Henry Young's conception of Christian faith is a form of humano-centric theism, according to William R. Jones. He thinks that process thinkers like Young adopt some variant of humanocentric theism.[119] Young would not oppose the labeling of his conception of God as

---

116. West, *Prophesy Deliverance!* 91.
117. West, *Prophetic Thought*, 43.
118. Ibid., 41–42.
119. Jones, "Process Theology," 277.

humanocentric, but I think that he would reject Jones's skepticism concerning humanocentric theism's potential to serve as an instrument and inspiration for liberation. He admits that the process view of God presents the future as open.[120] However, he contends that "God insures humanity's continual participation in the struggle for liberation."[121] How is this so? He asserts that while humans have the choice to refuse or reject courses of action, God nevertheless "aids the liberation process through the constant flow of inexhaustible possibilities into the world."[122] He points out that human freedom is conditioned but not determined.[123] I understand him to mean that human freedom must deal realistically with and sometimes work aggressively to assert itself against obstinate problems. Human freedom cannot be forever misguided or totally crushed or eliminated. Momentarily human freedom may be frustrated but is never disassociated from its potential.

## PINN AND ATHEISM

Through Anthony Pinn's distinction between weak and strong humanism, he challenges Jones's claim that humanocentric theism is the only rational alternative to black liberation theism. For Pinn, atheism is a rational alternative to black liberation theism and also humanocentric theism. Strong humanism results in a negative conception of Christian faith. According to Pinn, strong humanism has the following functions: "(1) it gives historical reign to humans; (2) it makes humanity the measure for all proofs; (3) it signifies or denies God's existence; (4) it operates according to an ethic of risk and is pragmatic in nature; and (5) it provides an ultimate concern related to community or human life."[124] He claims that it amounts to "an atheistic outlook which places humanity at the center of interest and activity."[125] For Pinn, therefore, strong humanism commends an atheistic position in black theology. As a strong humanist, he questions the existence of God and the use of Christian categories, namely, theodicy and the concept of redemptive suffering, in black liberation thought.

---

120. Young, *Hope in Process,* 136.
121. Henry J. Young, "Process Theology and Black Liberation: Testing the Whiteheadean Metaphysical Foundations," *Process Studies* 18, no. 4 (winter 1989): 266.
122. Young, *Hope in Process,* 129.
123. Ibid.
124. Pinn, *Why Lord?* 148.
125. Ibid.

## HUMAN-DETERMINED VALUE

Whether strong or weak, the humanism of the Black Philosophical School makes the individual, the human, the determiner of value. Neither God nor blackness, as in the Black Hermeneutical School, give value to liberation. For thinkers in the Black Philosophical School, liberation is ultimate because humans desire it. Anthony Pinn's interest in liberation actually leads him to deny the existence of God. He explains his position in the following manner:

> I could not accept the idea that the suffering of those I saw on a daily basis had any value at all. The oppressive circumstances church mothers discussed and stewards prayed about could not hold, for me, any merit in the struggle for "liberation." I needed to explore an alternative response that uncompromisingly affirms — at all costs, even the rejection of such concepts as the Christian view of God — the demonic nature of Black suffering. I believe that human liberation is more important than the maintenance of any religious symbol, sign, canon, or icon. It must be accomplished — both psychologically and physically — despite the damage done to cherished religious principles and traditions.[126]

For the sake of and for the cause of liberation, thinkers in the Black Philosophical School will accept or reject ideas on the basis of whether or not these ideas contribute of liberation, just as thinkers in the Black Hermeneutical School will do. However, for thinkers in the Black Hermeneutical School, liberation has a sacredness to it because it is supposedly the activity of God in the world. For thinkers in the Black Philosophical School, liberation is not anything sacred, but valuable because humans deem it so through their desire to achieve it. Liberation is a path toward the fulfillment of human nature and potential. Pinn's desire for and belief in the inherent good of liberation seems to be the principal and only validation that he needs for his work in academic black theology.

In my earlier discussion on the meaning of the term "black philosophy," I pointed out that blackness, at least in the way William R. Jones and Cornel West view it, is not normative, as it is in the Black

---

126. Ibid., 10–11.

Hermeneutical School. The humanist tradition, as West understands it, has no need to sacralize blackness in order to legitimate the study of African American life and culture. As he describes the tradition, it

> extols the distinctiveness of Afro-American culture and personality. It accents the universal human content of Afro-American cultural forms. It makes no ontological or sociological claims about Afro-American superiority or inferiority. Rather, it focuses on the ways in which creative Afro-American cultural modes of expression embody themes and motifs analogous to the vigorous cultural forms of other racial, ethnic, or national groups. This tradition affirms Afro-American membership in the human race, not above it or below it.[127]

## USE OF PHILOSOPHICAL SYSTEMS

Prevalent canons of university scholarship and the logical requirements of each thinker's preferred system of thought supplement the normative humanistic conceptions of Christian faith in the Black Philosophical School. In other words, theological claims are assessed by their coherence with propositions already established as true and notions of truth and rationality implied by a thinker's chosen system of philosophy.

According to Jones, black theology must adhere to commonly accepted logical canons. He insists that theological interpretation must minimally be internally consistent, systematically coherent, and free from both formal and informal fallacies of logic.[128] The normativity of humanism is evident in Jones's attempt to fashion Christian theism to accommodate humanism. As we have seen, Jones calls this wedding of theism and humanism "humanocentric theism." According to him, if black theologians accept this understanding of God and humanity, then they must acknowledge the logical constraints of this form of thinking about God and humanity.[129] I previously mentioned these constraints of humanocentric theism, as Jones outlined. The normativity of process metaphysics is seen in Henry Young's modification of traditional theological sources to conform with process

---

127. West, *Prophesy Deliverance!* 71.
128. Jones, *Is God a White Racist?* 175.
129. Ibid., 173–75, 194–97, 201–2.

metaphysics, which I discussed earlier.[130] Cornel West acknowledges the normativity of pragmatism. He is aware that his pragmatism presupposes an antifoundationalist theory of knowledge.[131] He accepts the antifoundationalist view that holds that claims to knowledge are adjudicated through the exercise of practical judgment in social situations. For West, logical argument alone does not settle intellectual disputes. The practical consequences of ideas suggest what is true.

## WALKER'S HUMANISM

The normativity of Alice Walker's humanism and construal of God is centered in her conception of womanism. As a widely read poet and novelist, she has influenced numerous persons. A considerable number of African American women in theological and religious studies base their understanding of feminism on her definition of "womanist," a term that she coined in 1983.[132] Her definition is divided into four parts. First, womanism refers to attributes such as maturity, assertiveness, curiosity, and seriousness. Second, it is a love for persons, sexually and/or non-sexually. Third, it is a love for self, life, culture, and the environment. Last, womanism is a form of feminism.

Alice Walker's humanism is undogmatic and vague, probably owing to the fact that she is not a professional academic theologian. Her humanism is a belief in human potential, dignity, free will, interrelationship, and mutual responsibility, based not in Christian theism but in a nature spirituality. She says,

> I seem to have spent all of my life rebelling against the church or other people's interpretations of what religion is — the truth is probably that I don't believe there is a God, although I would like to believe it. Certainly I don't believe there is a God beyond nature. The world is God. Man is God. So is a leaf or a snake.[133]

The conception of God that she can affirm is pantheistic. For Walker, God is the sum total of entities in the universe, but these entities each embody God. The universe is God. God is the principle of unity that unites as well as the spirit that animates all beings in nature.

---

130. Young, *Hope in Process*, 84–109.
131. West, *Keeping Faith*, 135–36.
132. Walker, *In Search of Our Mothers' Gardens*, xi–xii.
133. Ibid., 265.

Cheryl Sanders raises the issue of African American women in theology and ethics having adopted uncritically Alice Walker's concept of womanism. She points to three areas of conflict for African American women who are truly committed to a Christian circle of faith.[134] She notes, first of all, that Walker's womanism is based in humanism. In the Black Philosophical School, the fact of Walker's humanism poses no problem for black theology. However, for the Black Hermeneutical School, African American women must come to acknowledge the disparities between the humanistic orientation of Walker's womanism and black liberation theism. Second, according to Sanders, Walker's liberal views on sexuality are at odds with the church's traditional concept of heterosexual marriage and family life surrounding it. Third, her womanism represents an altogether autonomous framework of interpretation. Sanders seems to allude to the possibility that independent African American women's thought and scholarship in theology and ethics do not require grounding in Walker's womanism. Women in the Black Hermeneutical School have not explored sufficiently any other alternatives. They are unaware of the basic orientation of Walker's womanism — the black humanist tradition.

## METHOD

The methods of the Black Philosophical School are several. In contrast to thinkers in the Black Hermeneutical School, thinkers in the Black Philosophical School utilize empirical/descriptive analysis, philosophical analysis, biblical and philosophical hermeneutics, and deductive/logical argument. The humanistic norm of "functional ultimacy" — that is, emphasis on human freedom — influences methodology in the Black Philosophical School. Thinkers in the Black Philosophical School seem to use any type of critical method that promises to shed light on the issues of concern to them. The nature of philosophy may partly account for this plurality of methods. Philosophy does not seem to incorporate any particular method. The individual mind's arbitrary choice of which sources to use and which authorities to acknowledge guides the capacity to reason. Henry Young, Cornel West, and Anthony

---

134. Cheryl J. Sanders, "Christian Ethics and Theology in Womanist Perspective," in *Black Theology: A Documentary History, Volume Two: 1980–1992,* ed. Cone and Wilmore, 340–43.

Pinn identify and describe the methodologies most prevalent in their works. William R. Jones's method of internal criticism involves the use of philosophical analysis, logical argument, literary criticism, and biblical hermeneutics. His internal criticism is an assessment of black theology based on its principal category (i.e., theodicy) in light of its stated goal (i.e., black liberation). He critiques black theology "from the inside." Alice Walker's thought is expressed through the genres of poetry, novels, and occasionally nonfiction prose.

According to Henry Young, who is working principally within the context of Whitehead's process metaphysics, the method most appropriate to black liberation theology is empirical analysis, which supposedly is a method for analyzing and describing human experience as accurately as possible.[135] However, this task of descriptive analysis cannot be accomplished if one follows the traditional subject-object approach to empirical data, according to Young. He says that this subject-object approach is evident whenever "persons generally perceive themselves as subjects and view phenomena in the actual world as objects, standing over against themselves, to be interpreted.... Consequently, we relate to the phenomena as objects to be manipulated, controlled, and dominated."[136] He goes on to say:

> When the subject-object mode of thinking is incorporated into one's methodology, it leads to imposing one's presuppositions on the event being interpreted. These presuppositions can be both implicit and explicit. We need to be aware of both. In such instances, instead of allowing the authentic context of the event to unveil itself, the interpreter usually forces the event to conform to preconceived criteria of truth.[137]

Successful application of empirical analysis requires then, according to Young's terminology, the subject-subject approach. He contends that this approach safeguards against the distortion of sources, phenomena, or data being interpreted. "The subject-subject mode of thinking suggests that all things in the world... are inextricably bound together."[138] Inquirers using this mode of thought must recognize that

---

135. Young, *Hope in Process,* 77, 110.
136. Ibid., 81.
137. Ibid., 82.
138. Ibid., 83.

they are part of the same reality with the objects that they are interpreting and that these objects are subjects — that is, they have their own determination and worth apart from the inquirer's biases and presuppositions. Earlier in the section on sources in the Black Philosophical School, I discussed Young's views on how one must approach sources like experience, revelation, scripture, tradition, church history and culture, and reason to employ the empirical method in Whitehead's process metaphysics.

Not mere description only, the empirical method involves imaginative construction. Reciting Alfred North Whitehead's analogy to explain how the empirical method works in the advancement of knowledge, Henry Young says:

> He likens the true method of discovery to the flight of an airplane. It begins from the ground of empirical observation; it flies into the area of generalization and speculation. It then returns for renewed observation.[139]

Pragmatism supplies West with a fourfold method of hermeneutics, which he names using the terms "prophetic criticism," "cultural criticism," and "prophetic thought." According to Cornel West, his method of criticism is composed of four elements: (1) discernment, (2) connection, (3) tracking hypocrisy, and (4) hope.[140] By discernment, he means the analysis of contemporary situations in light of a complex past. This element in his method presupposes a form of historicism — that is, a view of history as the amalgamation of multiple social practices and cultural traditions.

An example of his exercise of discernment is found in his assertion of the existence of four African American traditions of response to white racism. The previous section on sources mentioned these traditions of response. By connection, he means empathy. An aim of his work is to deal with or express the anxieties and frustrations felt by people living in the Western world or adversely affected by its institutions and practices. Tracking hypocrisy involves exposing the gaps or inconsistencies between "principle and practice, between promise and performance, between rhetoric and reality." The element of hope is

---

139. Ibid., 77–78.
140. West, *Prophetic Thought,* 3–6.

his aim to believe personally and inspire other persons to believe that social transformation is possible and that humans have the capacity to achieve it. When applied, West contends that his method results in or contributes to "a genre of writing, a textuality, a mode of discourse that interprets, describes, and evaluates Afro-American life in order to comprehensively understand and effectively to transform it."[141] His method thus calls for the creation of a language for black liberation.

Anthony Pinn calls his methodology "nitty-gritty hermeneutics." His nitty-gritty hermeneutics is a form of philosophical hermeneutics that emerges from what he sees as a "strong, aggressive inquiry" that is irreverent to theistic religion and overlooks no cultural expression capable of bearing religious meanings.[142] He is advocating a form of interpretation that makes use only of philosophical analysis, deductive argument, empirical analysis, and other methods committed to the achievement of black liberation and the pursuit of truth, regardless of the direction such pursuit takes the inquirer. He says of his nitty-gritty hermeneutics:

> it holds no allegiance to Christian doctrine or theological sensibilities. It is not contaminated with nostalgic feelings toward traditional ways of viewing religious questions. Church tradition is less important than is the reality of oppression.[143]

His nitty-gritty hermeneutics reveals his suspicion of using Christian doctrinal structures and scripture for the interpretation of African American religion, which consists of modes of expression other than Christianity.

Using philosophical analysis, William R. Jones believes that he makes explicit that theodicy is the central category of black theology.[144] Anthony Pinn rejects theodicy because it is a Christian concept and leads to the false impression that it is the essential problem around which the interpretation of African American religion must revolve. More importantly, he sees theodicy as the enterprise of finding some redeeming quality in suffering. As I discussed earlier in the section

---

141. West, *Prophesy Deliverance!* 15.
142. Pinn, *Why Lord?* 114, 117, 180 n. 8.
143. Ibid., 19–20.
144. Jones, *Is God a White Racist?* xx–xxi; idem, "Theodicy: The Controlling Category for Black Theology," *Journal of Religious Thought* 30, no. 1 (spring–summer 1973): 28–29.

on sources, Pinn finds the notion of redemptive suffering unacceptable because, in the end, it justifies African Americans' sufferings by appeals to God's mysterious plans for the future.

## GOAL

Like the Black Hermeneutical School, the Black Philosophical School identifies as the goal of black theology moral and ethical action leading to liberation. Though clearly an intellectual activity, black theology presents itself as a strategy for liberation in the real world. Henry Young says emphatically that "We cannot afford to spiritualize oppression and relegate liberation to a compensatory orientation. Oppressed persons must be challenged to find fulfillment of their physical, emotional, and spiritual needs within history."[145] Because black theology is a form of liberation theology that is cognizant of the worst conditions under which people attempt to live, William R. Jones says that its ultimate goal must be the eradication of economic, social, and political oppression.[146] He goes on to say that black theology attains this goal by demonstrating unambiguously "that putting an end to oppression is a moral, spiritual, Christian, and biblical imperative."[147]

When pressed on the question about specific actions that one must perform in order to eliminate oppression, William R. Jones answers that moral and ethical action becomes obvious when one knows what oppression is, knows how it operates, and diagnoses accurately or identifies the causes contributing to situations of oppression. According to Jones, oppression consists of social differences that are arranged hierarchically; explained or justified by appeals to God (or religion), nature or some flaw in the victim of the oppression; and resulting in or supported by an imbalance in power between the oppressor and the victim.[148] He explains his position by saying:

---

145. Young, *Hope in Process,* 117–18.

146. William R. Jones, "Religion as Legitimator and Liberator: A Worm's Eye View of Religion and Contemporary Politics," in *Spirit Matters: The Worldwide Impact of Religion on Contemporary Politics,* ed. Richard L. Rubenstein (New York: Paragon House Publishers, 1986), 242.

147. Ibid.

148. William R. Jones, "Oppression, Race, and Humanism," *The Humanist* 52, no. 6 (November–December 1992): 8.

Oppression starts by highlighting a difference — either real or imagined. There are a lot of differences.... But what oppression always does is to arrange this difference in a hierarchy with a superior and an inferior. You don't have to respond to differences that way, but that's what oppression does. Then oppression will always justify that hierarchy. Wherever you find oppression, you have one group — the alleged superior group — with an overwhelming surplus of power, and another group — the alleged inferior group — with a clear-cut deficit.[149]

He goes on to point out that when God is cited as the cause of the oppression, the implication is: "If God made it, if God set up the inequality, then by definition it is good."[150] Nature is invoked to explain or justify inequality through the construction of physical descriptions of the world and entities in it. For example, as Cornel West points out, the pseudosciences of phrenology (the reading of skulls) and physiognomy (the reading of facial and bodily features) were used to explain the alleged inferiority of people of African descent and the alleged superiority of people of European descent.[151] He notes that Pieter Camper, a Dutch anatomist, asserted that the ideal facial angle was a one-hundred-degree angle exemplified by the ancient Greeks, whom he argued were a superior race physically and culturally. He showed that the facial angle of Europeans measured about ninety-seven degrees and that of African peoples between sixty and seventy degrees, near that of apes and dogs.

Jones contends that victims of oppression are blamed for their own oppression by the oppressing group's denial of the contextual dimension of causality. Here is how Jones explains the nature of causality:

I want to show you the distinction between what I call *initiating* cause and *consequent* cause. Imagine a row of dominos.... If I push the first domino, it's going to hit the second one, which in turn will hit the third, which will hit the fourth, and so forth. My first domino is my cause — my *initiating* cause — and when it hits the second domino and that domino moves, that's an effect,

149. Ibid.
150. Ibid.
151. West, *Prophesy Deliverance!* 56–58.

right? ... Domino two relative to domino three is what — cause or effect? It's cause, but it's the *consequent* cause. Please note that the same domino — the same event — can be both cause and effect, depending upon the context.[152]

Jones claims that Daniel P. Moynihan's *The Negro Family* (1965) contains an example of the subtle denial of the contextual dimension of causality. Moynihan asserts that the cause of the deterioration in the black community is caused by the breakdown in the black family. However, he says in his book that slavery is the cause of the deterioration in the black family. By minimizing attention on the initiating cause, slavery — a system maintained principally by and for whites, Moynihan removes whites from a large share of the responsibility for the conditions under which blacks currently live. He makes blacks themselves the cause of their own plight.

For William R. Jones, action must be taken on two fronts in order to achieve liberation. The first front is the intellectual level, in the realm of ideas. For Jones, action on this level is aimed at gnosiological conversion. As I mentioned earlier under the section on tasks of black theology, gnosiological conversion is a term that Jones uses to describe the liberation of black people's minds from bondage to the system of beliefs that give support and justification to oppression.

The second front is deliberate social action. As I mentioned earlier, in the section of this chapter on content in the Black Philosophical School, Jones's conception of liberation is contextual. He does not believe that liberating social action must take any particular form. For him, liberation is not necessarily integration, socialism, nationalism, and so forth. Jones does believe that persons must engage in social action aimed at correcting power imbalances, but his recommendation is based on what his interpretation of oppression is: an imbalance in power that is justified by a system of beliefs. After attacking this system of ideas, one must deal with the inequities between whites and blacks. How does one reduce or eradicate the power imbalance? Jones's answer is, "Accurate diagnosis of the situation." Liberating social action is whatever works for a given situation. In contrast to Jones, West believes that Antonio Gramsci's neo-Marxism, that I discussed earlier,

---

152. Jones, "Oppression, Race, and Humanism," 32.

is a form of social analysis which leads to an accurate description of oppression and therefore recommendations for liberating actions.

Cornel West contends that African American churches must play a role in achieving liberation; he does not believe, however, that these institutions by themselves can change American society.[153] The church has no monopoly on ethical values and deeds.[154] Other institutions such as schools, families, mass media (television, newspaper, movies, etc.), which communicate values and become a context for social action, can help usher in change, according to West. He thinks that churches must undergo radical restructuring and then join in coalitions with other institutions committed to the task of creating governmental programs that will effect change on a broad scale — at least in areas beyond the domains of each separate institution. The many things that church leaders must do in order to restructure their churches include: (1) use social and political analysis, especially Marxism, in order to accurately describe and diagnose situations of injustice; (2) stimulate economic development in black communities; (3) become financially accountable through truth and openness in financial transactions and record-keeping; (4) organize viable ministries; (5) become self-critical, scrutinizing themselves and their churches, and close the gaps between principles and practices; (6) work with governmental agencies; and (7) become more democratic and inclusive in church membership, ministry, worship, and so forth.[155]

In West's opinion, not only black churches but all other institutions must (1) develop a new language or way of talking for heightening persons' awareness of what oppression is; (2) focus attention on the common good, that is, on matters of concern to all peoples and that which is in the best interest of them all; (3) develop programs for large-scale governmental intervention to ensure access to the goods and services of society; (4) engage in grassroots organizing based on democratic life and ideals; and (5) maintain hope or optimism in the capacity of humans to solve the problems facing their lives.[156] They must never lose faith that liberation can be achieved.

---

153. West, *Prophetic Thought*, 23–26.
154. Cornel West, *Prophetic Reflections: Notes on Race and Power in America*, vol. 2, *Beyond Eurocentrism and Multiculturalism* (Monroe, Maine: Common Courage Press, 1993), 106.
155. Ibid., 73–80.
156. Cornel West, *Race Matters* (Boston: Beacon Press, 1993), 6–8.

Alice Walker believes in change, personal and social.[157] She also believes that responsible ethical action may take several forms.[158] Her personal choice has been to deal with injustice through her writing. She does not equate her writing with the heroism of leaders in civil rights movements and organizations, but her exercise of choice reflects an awareness of social responsibility. Her insistence on the freedom of the individual to choose her own course is not a retreat from social activism but is an aspect of her nature that she affirms; she cannot and does not deny that she has the capacity to make choices. The choice of what to do or what not to do rests ultimately with the individual. Whatever she does, she makes clear, "it will be My Choice."[159]

## SUMMARY

William R. Jones, Cornel West, Anthony Pinn, and Henry Young's shared methodological perspective becomes pronounced when one examines their views on the tasks, content, sources, norm, method, and goal of academic black theology. Alice Walker is not a scholar in religion per se, but her conception of womanism has influenced many African American women in theological and religious studies and is capable of classification as a form of black humanism.

Thinkers in the Black Philosophical School accept the Black Hermeneutical School's assertion that the tasks of black theology are description, analysis, evaluation, explanation, construction, and revision. However, they tend to place emphasis on the task of revision. Jones calls this task of revision "gnosiological conversion." Based upon his understanding of oppression as social inequality explained and justified by a system of beliefs or ideas and granting power to an allegedly superior group in order to institutionalize its prejudices and advantages, the criticism and reconstruction of ideas is a crucial and first step in the achievement of liberation.

All thinkers agree that liberation is the content of black theology. They do not rely as much on the Bible and black folk story in order to explain liberation. Instead, they define liberation using social and political philosophies that may or may not be compatible with the Bible

---

157. Walker, *In Search of Our Mothers' Gardens*, 252.
158. Ibid., 168–70.
159. Ibid., 170.

or black story. For Jones, liberation is contextual. The meaning of liberation as well as the means for achieving it result from the unique historical situation of an oppressed population. Pinn defines liberation as a vision of life leading to great opportunities for individual fulfillment and a better sense and appreciation of human worth. West defines liberation as overcoming capitalism and the myriad of social ills that accompany it. Young defines liberation as a state of cultural pluralism where various social groups coexist peacefully and each possess the privilege of self-realization. For Walker, black liberation is integration of the sort that Martin Luther King Jr espoused.

As with the Black Hermeneutical School, the black experience, in all of its multiple dimensions, is a source for theological reflection in the Black Philosophical School. Walker emphasizes African American women's experience and culture. Other sources include revelation, scripture, tradition, church history and culture, and reason. Young discusses how these sources must be modified in order to satisfy what he understands as the logical constraints of process metaphysics, which is a source of reason that sets apart the Black Philosophical School from other schools in black theology. Common to Young, West, Pinn, and Jones is reason in the form of philosophical traditions. Humanism is the principal philosophical tradition utilized in the theological reflection of Jones and Pinn. Walker's womanism is a form of humanism. Young utilizes process metaphysics. West's thinking is informed greatly by pragmatism.

The norm of the Black Philosophical School is found in humanistic conceptions of Christian faith; thinkers in the Black Philosophical School ground academic black theology in humanism. Pinn distinguishes between weak and strong versions of humanism. His distinction is helpful in explaining how the normativity of humanism results in conceptions of Christian faith that are both positive and negative. Jones, Young, and West, as weak humanists, in various ways modify or affirm Christian faith, but Pinn, as a strong humanist, denies its authority altogether in academic scholarship and black liberation. While Walker vacillates between atheism and agnosticism with respect to the traditional Judeo-Christian conception of God, she is committed to a pantheistic spirituality, the belief that God is the unity that underlies as well as the spirit that animates each living thing that embodies God. God is identical with nature.

The normativity of humanism prohibits the black experience from being normative. African American humanists neither sacralize blackness in order to legitimate the study of African American life and culture nor do they sacralize liberation as the sole activity of God in order to justify the attention they give to it. Humanists emphasize African Americans' membership in the human race, not above it or below it. Liberation is valuable because humans deem it so through their desire to achieve it. The normativity of humanism is supplemented by prevalent canons of university scholarship and the logical requirements of each thinkers' preferred system of thought. That is to say, the assessment of theological claims is tested by their coherence with propositions already established as true as well as notions of truth and rationality implied by a thinker's chosen system of philosophy.

Thinkers in the Black Philosophical School utilize a variety of methods, such as empirical/descriptive analysis, philosophical analysis, biblical and philosophical hermeneutics, and deductive/logical argument. Their choices of method seem to be based on what each presupposes is the best method that will shed light on the issues of concern to him or her. Young accepts empirical analysis as the method of process theology. He also accepts biblical hermeneutics and other methods when they are compatible with empirical method in process theology. West utilizes a program of philosophical hermeneutics that he calls by the names "prophetic criticism," "cultural criticism," and "prophetic thought." Pinn subscribes to a program of philosophical hermeneutics that he calls "nitty-gritty hermeneutics." Submitting to no authority other than reason, his nitty-gritty hermeneutics comes out of a tenacious pursuit of the truth. One can see in Jones's internal criticism his use of philosophical analysis, logical argument, literary criticism, and biblical hermeneutics. Walker's thought is expressed through the genres of poetry, novels, and occasionally nonfiction prose.

Each thinker sees moral and ethical action as the goal of black theology. They are not all unconcerned about knowledge as a goal of inquiry. For example, West believes his method contributes to a genre of writing that interprets, describes, and evaluates Afro-American life while seeking to transform it. West believes that African American churches play an important role in achieving change. Yet, these institutions, he believes, must work in conjunction with other institutions (family, schools, communication industries, government, etc.) in order to liberate oppressed peoples. Based on Jones's understanding of what he thinks oppression is, liberating action amounts to attacking the system of ideas that justify oppression and correcting imbalances in power existing between social or ethnic groups. In either case, Jones believes that liberating action will require accurate descriptions of oppressive ideas and situations of injustice. West believes that he has found a method of accurate social analysis in Antonio Gramsci's neo-Marxism. Walker underscores the role of personal choice in determining what is appropriate, socially responsible action.

# CHAPTER FOUR

# The Human Sciences School

J AMES H. CONE'S *Black Theology and Black Power* (1969) and *A Black Theology of Liberation* (1970) defined several issues around which debates among black theologians occurred.[1] One of those issues was the nature of black religion and its relation to black theology as the latter's proper subject matter. According to Cone himself, the most formidable and influential discussant in this debate was Charles H. Long.[2] As Cone understood him, Long was contending that the history of religions is "the best tool for examining black religion."[3]

Actually, Long's intention is to chart an alternative methodological perspective to what he sees as the two most dominant and narrow approaches to the study and interpretation of African American religion. He contends that basically two kinds of studies of African American religion exist: sociological and theological/apologetic.[4] Examples of the kinds of sociological studies that he has in mind are W. E. B. Du Bois's *The Negro Church* (1903), Carter G. Woodson's *The History of the Negro Church* (1921), Benjamin E. Mays and Joseph W. Nicholson's *The Negro's Church* (1933), Arthur H. Fauset's *Black Gods of the Metropolis* (1944), C. Eric Lincoln's *Black Muslims in America* (1961), E. U. Essien-Udom's *Black Nationalism* (1962), E. Franklin Frazier's *The Negro Church in America* (1963), and Howard Brotz's *The Black Jews of Harlem* (1970).[5] In his opinion, these studies have not "come to terms with the specifically religious elements in the religion of black Americans."[6] In other words, these studies deal mostly

---

1. Cone, "An Interpretation of the Debate among Black Theologia..s," Epilogue to *Black Theology: A Documentary History, 1966–1979,* ed. Cone and Wilmore, 612.

2. Ibid., 615.

3. Cone, *My Soul Looks Back,* 60.

4. Charles H. Long, *Significations: Signs, Symbols, and Images in the Interpretation of Religion* (Philadelphia: Fortress Press, 1986), 173.

5. Ibid., 183 n. 1.

6. Ibid., 173.

with the history, organization, experiences, and political ideologies of African American communities. Rarely do they identify and examine the images and meanings of religious significance to these communities. The theological studies that Long has in mind are Joseph Washington's *Black Religion* (1964), Albert Cleage's *The Black Messiah* (1968), James Cone's *Black Theology and Black Power* (1969), and subsequent interpretive works on black religion.[7] According to him, these studies are aimed at defending and legitimating the existence of a religious tradition, namely, black religion, that differs significantly from the mainstream of American religion.

Using Washington's book in order to illustrate the limitation of theological/apologetic works, he points out that the severe restriction of these kinds of studies is their inability "to deal with religion outside of the normative framework of Christian theology."[8] In contrast to the theological/apologetic and sociological approaches, he contends that the history of religions approach does not obligate scholars to equate their studies with or defend Christianity, or any other religion for that matter.[9] Instead, this approach is committed to the identification and exploration of religious images, symbols, and meanings of significance to various African American communities, whether Christian, non-Christian, or secular.

I name the methodological perspective initiated by Charles Long "the Human Sciences School." He considers the history of religions to be one of the human sciences.[10] He understands the human sciences to be disciplines related to various aspects and existential problems of human civilization. For example, he contends that economics is related to the problems of production and class structuring, psychology to sexuality and loss of meaning, and the study of religion to humanity's place in the world.[11]

In addition to the history of religions, economics, and psychology, the human sciences includes other fields such as sociology, anthropology, history, and religious studies.[12] I have read nowhere of Charles Long's advocating the history of religions approach as the only legiti-

---

7. Ibid.
8. Ibid., 174.
9. Ibid.
10. Ibid., 73.
11. Ibid., 91, 97–98.
12. Ibid., 66, 73, 76.

mate alternative to sociological and theological/apologetic studies that overlook or conceal the full range of religious meanings in African American religion and culture. I think that he would be open to approaches from other human science disciplines. His approach is not opposed to sociological study, theology, or philosophy. His criticism is against the manner in which scholars (black and nonblack) in the liberal arts (humanities and social sciences) have treated African American religion and culture — denying, overlooking, or masking its full range of religious meanings. Though Charles Long's primary locus for the study and interpretation of African American religion is from the perspective of the history of religions, the term "human sciences" is a covering term for the kinds of cultural studies that he is recommending.

Whereas the Black Philosophical School embraces particularism — that is, taking an ethnic approach to a discipline — the Human Sciences School acknowledges universalism in existing academic disciplines. In the Black Hermeneutical School, arguments are made for the legitimacy of black theology based on the neglect of black experience as a source of theological reflection in the history of Western Christianity. In the Black Philosophical School, William R. Jones argues for the inclusion of black theology because it will contribute to philosophy's goal of describing reality. Because reality cannot be grasped by one viewpoint alone, Jones asserts that multiple perspectives are needed, including black theology.

For Charles Long, no arguments for the uniqueness of African American religion or its neglect by white scholars, which may well be true, are necessary to warrant studying black theology. From an approach altogether different than Jones's, Long endorses the study of African American religion because the nature of his academic discipline, the history of religions, permits just that — the study of religions. Long therefore contends that the history of religions contains a universalism that provides an opening for the study of the authentic religious expression of all peoples.[13] As a study of the religious beliefs of African Americans, black theology is automatically a part of the study of religion. As a study in the field of religion, the study of black theology has a legitimate place in the human sciences of the university.

---

13. Ibid., 8.

## THINKERS

In addition to Charles Long, Cheryl Townsend Gilkes, C. Eric Lincoln, Henry Mitchell, Charles Shelby Rooks, and Theophus Smith are thinkers capable of classification within the Human Sciences School of academic black theology. According to both James Cone and Gayraud Wilmore, the Society for the Study of Black Religion (SSBR) represents the second stage of and a major arena for discussions on black theology.[14] The society organized under the leadership of Rooks. Both Rooks and Long, and even Wilmore, served as presidents of the SSBR.[15] Long and Rooks are "friendly critics" of Cone. In acknowledging the influence of Long and Rooks on his thinking and especially in the publication of his book *For My People,* Cone says:

> Charles H. Long and C. Shelby Rooks are special friends who also have been very supportive of my work for many years. They gave my manuscript a critical reading, correcting some misleading statements and offering their judgment regarding the strengths and weaknesses of my interpretation of black theology's history and my suggestions for its future development.[16]

Henry Mitchell has a long history of involvement in the contemporary black theological movement. Prior to the formation of the SSBR, Mitchell was a member of the Theological Commission of the National Conference of Black Churchmen (NCBC), the first arena for discussions on contemporary black theology. Along with Cone, Preston Williams, and J. Deotis Roberts, he contributed to the NCBC's first public statement on black theology at its 1969 meeting in Atlanta, Georgia.[17] Also, he was the first director and Martin Luther King Jr. Memorial Professor of Black Church Studies at Colgate-Rochester Divinity School, the first such program in a predominately white theological school in the United States.[18] Mitchell contends that, since the days of his study at Union Theological Seminary under Paul Tillich, he has been concerned principally with research and teaching on religious

---

14. Cone, *For My People,* 26; Wilmore, General Introduction to *Black Theology: A Documentary History, 1966–1979,* ed. Cone and Wilmore, 5.

15. Rooks, *Revolution in Zion,* 135, 136, 145, 146.

16. Cone, *For My People,* xii.

17. Wilmore, *Black Religion and Black Radicalism,* 2d ed., 215.

18. Gayraud S. Wilmore, Foreword to Henry H. Mitchell's *Black Belief: Folk Beliefs of Blacks in America and West Africa* (New York: Harper & Row, 1975), xi.

beliefs in culture.[19] He takes a cultural studies approach to the study of African American religion that is compatible with Charles Long's history of religions approach to black theology. For him, the study of culture automatically includes the study of the culture and religion of African Americans. As I discuss, he contends that no people exist who lack culture or religious beliefs.

Theophus Smith locates his study of African American spirituality within the field of religious studies.[20] He claims that the history of religions and black liberation theology has influenced his study. He says that he draws upon approaches and methods in the human sciences or cultural studies.[21] In his own words, he says:

> As one among other scholars engaged in the nascent field of African American spirituality, I locate its interests somewhere between the historical and social science study of religion on the one hand, and the black theology of liberation on the other, spanning literary and aesthetic considerations in between. A convergence of interest in spirituality as a distinctive category of religious phenomena can be observed, first, from the religious studies side.[22]

Cheryl Gilkes and C. Eric Lincoln are sociologists of religion who recognize the depth of religious meanings in African American life and seek to influence how these meanings are interpreted theologically. Gilkes is a foremost womanist scholar in the sociology of African American religion. She participates in forums that are shaping womanist-oriented studies in theology and ethics. Lincoln is considered the "dean" of contemporary black church and religious studies.[23] He is the leading sociologist of African American religion since E. Franklin Frazier. Lincoln participated in the Theological Commission of the NCBC and has been an active member of the SSBR. Besides his work as a professor of sociology and religion in the late '60s at Union Theological Seminary and since the mid-'70s as a professor

---

19. Henry H. Mitchell and Nicholas Cooper-Lewter, *Soul Theology: The Heart of American Black Culture* (San Francisco: Harper & Row, 1986), xiii–xiv.

20. Theophus H. Smith, *Conjuring Culture: Biblical Formations of Black America* (New York: Oxford University Press, 1994), ix.

21. Ibid., 10.

22. Ibid., ix.

23. Cone, *For My People*, 74.

of religion and culture at Duke University, he edited a series on black religion that made possible the publication of books by numerous African American scholars in theology and religion.

Cheryl Gilkes, C. Eric Lincoln, Charles Long, Henry Mitchell, Charles Rooks, and Theophus Smith are not prolific writers in systematic theology. They approach the study of African American religion from their respective human and social science disciplines. In the course of their works, they have made proposals that, if taken seriously and pursued, will result in a construction of black theology that differs from those in the Black Hermeneutical and Black Philosophical schools.

## TASKS

In the Human Sciences School, the tasks of black theology are not unlike the proposed tasks of black theology in the Black Hermeneutical and Black Philosophical schools. In all schools, black theology involves description, analysis, explanation, revision, and construction. Like James Evans of the Black Hermeneutical School, Charles Long prefers to use the term "deconstruction" in place of the term "revision." Long has been most vocal in support of revision and rejection of imaginative speculation. He, along with Henry Mitchell, embraces construction, provided that it is approached inductively.

According to Charles Long, black theology must begin first with the task of revision. Black theology is one of several possible opaque theologies.[24] A people's experiences of reality are "opaque" by virtue of the unique quality of their experiences that differ significantly and stand apart from the experiences of other people. The opacity of black theology results from African Americans' experience of oppression but discovery of beauty, meaning, and worth in human life.[25] Opaque theologies represent a mode of human being, a way of experiencing and living, thinking, and enduring the harshness of life.

According to Long, the opacity of religion is rarely acknowledged. The religion of oppressed people is usually overlooked and not given serious scholarly consideration. As an opaque theology, black

24. Long, *Significations,* 193ff.
25. Ibid., 195.

theology must begin with the misinterpretations of the religious experiences of oppressed peoples. Along with the deconstruction of these misinterpretations, black theology must intensely search for more substantive and plausible interpretations of religious meanings in the life experiences of oppressed peoples.[26]

Charles Long's understanding of the revisionist task of black theology parallels William R. Jones's notion of gnosiological conversion. Gnosiological conversion calls for a fundamental restructuring of oppressed blacks' present worldview and lifestyles. Long's notion of deconstruction envisions nothing less than a change in the thinking and actions of oppressed people whose oppressors usually circumscribe their identity.

Charles Long is doubtful and suspicious of constructive black theology. He contends that theology, in a traditional Western sense, presupposes the will to power.[27] He thinks that this will to power rests upon a narrow definition of religion. He says:

In the strict sense of the word, theology may be understood as a discourse and study within a narrowly limited context. Such a context would be restricted to the doctrine, teachings, liturgical practices, and historical formulations of a particular religious tradition. The aims of theology within this context are to clarify, enhance, and extend through serious thought, reflection, and practice the meaning and ministry of the specific religious tradition.[28]

This definition of theology is not Long's. This definition binds theology to the task of promoting a particular religion as opposed to contributing to what he thinks is the greater task of understanding the role of religion in human societies. According to Long, scholars of religion have for too long allowed the American Protestant Christian tradition to shape their understanding of theology. He believes that scholars' definition and understanding of the scope of theology will

26. Ibid., 136, 142, 154, 195.
27. Charles H. Long, as interpreted in Cone's "An Interpretation of the Debate among Black Theologians," Epilogue to *Black Theology: A Documentary History, 1966–1979*, ed. Cone and Wilmore, 616.
28. Charles H. Long, "A Common Ancestor: Theology and Religious Studies," in *Religious Studies, Theological Studies, and the University-Divinity School*, ed. Joseph Kitagawa (Atlanta: Scholars Press, 1992), 137.

change as the meaning of religion changes to respectfully acknowledge the plurality of religions in the world.[29]

For Charles Long, the appropriate task of theology is description. He understands description as the structuring of phenomena that enables persons to communicate and learn an existing worldview. As he understands the history of religions approach, the inquirer's task is to put the religious expressions of a people into a structured system or ordered language.[30] However, in so doing, the inquirer is not suggesting or inventing a worldview. The structure or language of description is a bridge between the inquirer and the persons whose religious beliefs and practices are being studied.

From an altogether different approach, Henry Mitchell is critical of the normal method of theological construction. Theological construction usually starts with a corpus of doctrinal assumptions and reasons deductively from them, according to Mitchell.[31] He recognizes as better his own approach of commencing theological interpretation with a people's core beliefs — that is, those beliefs in a religion which people actually adhere to and utilize in their lives. Identifying and describing these core beliefs is necessary. Mitchell's approach is empirical and inductive, taking nothing for granted but considering and examining various beliefs that eventually add up to a coherent system.[32] He claims that this coherent system is not his invention or suggestion on what persons ought to believe but the actual arrangement of beliefs reflected in the case studies of persons whom he has observed. Charles Long's insistence on the structuring of religious beliefs using methods of thorough description is compatible with Mitchell's concept of an inductive approach to theological construction. Both thinkers are opposed to the inquirer's inventing or suggesting beliefs that have not been proven empirically to exist in a religious community.

As C. Eric Lincoln seeks to clarify his role as a sociologist of religion, he distinguishes the tasks of the theologian from those of the sociologist. As a sociologist, he deals with quantitative distinctions, observable and measurable phenomena. He leaves to the theologian the interpretation of qualitative matters involving the ways and means that

---

29. Ibid., 149.
30. Long, *Significations,* 46.
31. Mitchell and Lewter, *Soul Theology,* 6.
32. Ibid., 11.

persons structure their experiences of reality. Ultimate reality — that which is of importance with respect to whether and how persons live or die — is mediated through symbols.[33] The theologian must clarify and interpret these symbols as people undergo historical change.[34]

Lincoln calls the "black sacred cosmos" the network of symbols that African Americans use.[35] While objects and figures and the emphasis given to each will vary from one religious tradition to the next, in the black sacred cosmos, God, Christ, freedom, Spirit, and personal conversion are the principal symbols and concepts around which other religious meanings coalesce.[36] By interpreting these symbols, the theologian makes black religion meaningfully understood by people engaged in it, people aware or not aware of it, and people who deny its existence or oppose its operation. While the theologian's and sociologist's works may be mutually supportive, theological statements are not verified through sociological study, according to Lincoln.[37] Theology has its own methods of study and system of verification.

## CONTENT

In the Human Sciences School, the content of black theology is empowerment. Thinkers in the Human Sciences School agree that black theology contributes to the task of restructuring the conditions of human life. No thinker wishes to limit the notion of change to liberation from economic, social, and political oppression. The term "empowerment" best suits these thinkers. Theophus Smith does not think that black theology should be limited to the theme of liberation, as in the case of the Black Hermeneutical and Black Philosophical schools.[38] He may not be aware that, in the Black Hermeneutical School, Olin Moyd's concept of redemption as liberation and confederation is similar to the notion of empowerment in the Human Sciences School. At any rate, he contends that African American religion is magic, a quest for power and control over various aspects of

33. C. Eric Lincoln, *The Black Church since Frazier* (New York: Schocken Books, 1974), 137–38.

34. Ibid.

35. Lincoln and Mamiya, *The Black Church in the African American Experience*, 2.

36. Ibid., 3–7.

37. C. Eric Lincoln, "Contemporary Black Religion: In Search of a Sociology," *Journal of the Interdenominational Theological Center* 5, no. 2 (spring 1978): 96.

38. Smith, *Conjuring Culture*, 178–79.

life that constitute their reality.[39] Thus for Smith, magic, or conjure as he prefers to call it, is a form and strategy for empowerment.

Henry Mitchell's examination of core beliefs among African Americans focuses on how these beliefs empower and sustain African Americans in the face of life's difficulties, not only in situations of oppression but also in times of loneliness, bereavement, divorce, sickness, and so forth. Black theology deals with the religious meanings that have empowered African Americans through their experiences of what Charles Long calls the "hardness of life."[40] According to him, black theology is created during moments of crisis as African Americans have reflected on their religious beliefs. The beliefs of the people that survive intense questioning usually are those beliefs that leave them with an appreciation of life despite life's being at times hard and unbearable.

While C. Eric Lincoln agrees that religion is multifaceted, he contends that black religion's aim and essential commitment is to destroy caste in America.[41] Liberation is not the sole aim of religion per se, but it does have an exalted status over other themes in African American religion. Lincoln defines liberation as "the restoration of dignity, the negation of violence" and violence as "[compromising] the humanity of another."[42] While perhaps exploring a variety of themes, a theologian must not assume that his scholarly interests establish the importance of the meanings that one wishes to study and interpret. Lincoln says, as a matter of fact, the dehumanization of persons by social stratification by race, class, sex, and so forth in American society has given liberation the importance that it has in African American religion.

## SOURCES

In the Human Sciences School, the sources of black theology are black religion and culture, each of which is understood as a complex system of thought and action that serves to orient persons to the ultimate significance of their place in the world. Charles Long, for example,

---

39. Ibid., 4.
40. Long, *Significations,* 193.
41. Lincoln, *The Black Church since Frazier,* 135.
42. Ibid., 147.

understands religion as a complex cultural phenomenon that involves various experiences, expressions, motivations, intentions, behaviors, styles, rhythms, and structures of thought.[43] The sources of black theology also include the histories and traditions of African Americans — that is, modes of experience and expression that reveal their inner and intimate lives.[44]

In addition to this broad definition of religion that may encompass meanings that are not overtly religious, religion is not restricted to Christianity only, according to Long. He contends that Christian churches are not the only context of religion among African Americans. He says:

> The Christian religion provided a language for the meaning of religion but not all the religious meanings of the black community were encompassed by the Christian forms of religion . . . as those forms are contained in folklore, music, style of life, and so on. Some tensions have existed between these forms of orientation and those of the Christian churches, but some of these extra-church orientations have had great critical and creative power. They have often touched deeper religious issues regarding the true situation of black communities than those of the church leaders of their time.[45]

Long's point is that: the sources of African American religion may, of course, be found not only in Christian churches but also in other religions, folklore, music, lifestyles, and systems of thought that are not always dependent upon or complimentary to Christianity.

For C. Eric Lincoln, the proper subject matter of black theology is black religion. A very important dimension of culture, religion expresses and legitimates, sometimes challenges, the core beliefs, practices, and values of a society.[46] Our most intimate view of a people is through their religion, which discloses "a lot about their politics, their social habits, their fears, their failures, their understanding of who they are and what life holds for them."[47] To know American so-

---

43. Long, *Significations*, 7.
44. Ibid., 195.
45. Ibid, 7.
46. Lincoln and Mamiya, *The Black Church in the African American Experience*, 7; Lincoln, *The Black Church since Frazier*, 135.
47. Lincoln, *The Black Church since Frazier*, 104.

ciety generally and black culture particularly, one must study religion. Black religion is diverse, as Lincoln knows. While his *The Black Muslims in America* (1961) remains a classic text on Islam among African Americans, he has focused most of his studies on black Christianity, namely, black evangelical Protestantism. After all, the black sacred cosmos, the religious worldview of African Americans, is mediated through Judeo-Christian symbols, according to Lincoln.

Cheryl Gilkes as well studies black Christianity but with a special focus on women's experience and how it shapes the culture and consciousness of African Americans. She explores women's experiences on a variety of subjects, including leadership roles (religious and secular), music, education, food, family life, beauty norms, biblical interpretation, and feminine imagery and metaphor.

The principal source of theology is what Henry Mitchell calls core beliefs. He contends that "all cultures have clusters of core convictions about reality."[48] He says

> everybody everywhere does have beliefs. Nobody, in politics or out of it, makes decisions in a religious vacuum. Everybody has a belief system out of which all value judgments flow. Unuttered or expressed, an assumption inescapably involving some sort of faith determines all conscious choices and influences all unthinking response.[49]

Mitchell says that these core beliefs are

> the bedrock attitudes that govern all deliberate behavior and relationships and also spontaneous responses to crises.... [T]hey are not inherited or beyond the influences of training and spiritual discipline. They have been acquired through life experiences, worship, and cultural exposure, and they can be altered likewise. Core beliefs are not mere propositions to which assent is given. They are the ways one trusts or fails to trust. They are embraced intuitively and emotionally, with or without the ability to express them rationally.[50]

---

48. Mitchell and Cooper-Lewter, *Soul Theology,* ix.
49. Ibid., 1.
50. Ibid., 3.

The cluster of core beliefs that he sees at the heart of African American culture are belief in the providence, justice, majesty and omnipotence, omniscience, goodness, and grace of God; belief in the equality of persons; belief in the obligation of persons to persevere suffering; belief in the parenthood of God and the kinship of all peoples; and belief that life is good and worth living.

African American religion has no absolute, unique black essence. For Henry Mitchell, black religion is black not because of some unique essence. Black religion is black because a substantial number of African Americans have similar beliefs and experiences. He says:

> The existence of a black theological style and content does not hang on its uniqueness. It hangs, rather, on whether or not there are an experience and an interpretation of it that (taken as a whole) is sufficiently different in its balance and emphases from other racial and class-group interpretations to be reasonably identified as belonging to at least a majority of black Christians, as opposed to a majority of another race and/or class.[51]

Charles Long contends that black religion is African in its origin, although he argues that it must be viewed as part of the total American religious history.[52] Black religion has, as a distinctive feature, its use of Western categories: biblical motifs, metaphors, christology, and so forth. The fact of a heritage does not bar black religion from dynamic relationship with other religious traditions found in American life and culture. Long seems to be saying that black religion does not exist in a cultural vacuum.

Still regarding African American religion as the chief source for black theology, Theophus Smith looks to a variety of sources to aid him in analyzing and interpreting African American religion. He describes his studies as interdisciplinary. Smith says that he weaves into a single focus "disciplinary approaches and methods drawn from the human sciences or cultural studies. The disciplines involved include the history of religions and social history, literary criticism and critical theory, ethnography and ethnomusicology, and phenomenology and

---

51. Henry H. Mitchell, "The Theological Posits of Black Christianity," in *Black Theology II: Essays on the Formation and Outreach of Contemporary Black Theology,* ed. Calvin E. Bruce and William R. Jones (Lewisburg, Pa.: Bucknell University Press, 1978), 118.

52. Long, *Significations,* 148–55.

biblical hermeneutics."[53] Smith does not seem to think that religious data interprets itself. After identifying and qualifying one's data from a religion, one must determine how best to analyze and evaluate it. He exercises the prerogative to make use of any and all disciplinary and methodological sources that he believes will contribute to his analysis and evaluation of African American religion.

In my best estimate of Henry Mitchell's work, sources of influence in his work include systematic theology, clinical psychology, biblical hermeneutics, and ethnomusicology (study of African American music).

## NORM

The norm of the Human Sciences School is phenomenological conceptions of religion and prevailing academic canons of rationality and truth. Like the Black Philosophical School, the Human Sciences School turns to a foundation external to African American religion in order to assert the intelligibility of black theology. The Black Hermeneutical School is nonfoundational, asserting that black Christian faith requires no grounding because it has its own logic and truth. Whereas the Black Philosophical School turns to humanism, the Human Sciences School turns to phenomenology.

Phenomenology attempts to describe religions and religious themes as they appear or function in the life and consciousness of the people who participate in a religion. Theophus Smith and Henry Mitchell explain the phenomenological approach to African American religion. Smith says about his study in African American spirituality:

> This is a phenomenological presentation. By "phenomenological" I mean a description of this occurrence as it "gives itself" in actual experience, prior to any attempt to schematize or classify it. Thus I intend to "bracket" all valuational or categorical considerations. . . . Similarly, I will resist . . . any pressure to locate this phenomenon in relation to the Christian dogma (a premature consideration whenever systematic theologians and religious

---

53. Smith, *Conjuring Culture*, 10.

thinkers seek to organize occurrences without first allowing the phenomenon to reveal its inner dynamism).[54]

Mitchell says about his approach to the study of core beliefs:

> [they] must be stated in the terms in which ordinary folk state them, when they are verbalized at all. . . . I must not "fight their feeling" and style, in the interest of scholarly credibility. If a widely used phrase comes from a fundamentalist hymn dear to the black brethren, I must tell it like it is believed and felt, even though there is on my agenda an item about acculturating people away from some of the unfortunate lyrics that go along with the profoundly nourishing items.[55]

Mitchell and Smith explain the phenomenological approach as the most objective approach to the study of African American religion. This approach supposedly presents religion as it is or actually manifests and operates in the lives of people. In my discussion on the content of academic black theology in the Human Sciences School, I mentioned that Mitchell, Smith, and Long are convinced that African American religion, as it is and how most African Americans are aware of it, functions to empower persons in the face of life's difficulties. Lincoln does not believe that black religion is indiscriminate about life's difficulties. He contends that historical and social circumstances cause black religion to view caste as the major difficulty in life for African Americans to overcome.

The phenomenological approach and goal of objectivity in the Human Sciences School accords no special authority to blackness. Long argues against the portrayal of blackness as an ontological symbol. In the Black Hermeneutical School, James Cone claims that blackness is an ontological symbol which points to a transcendent reality and truth, namely, God's character and activity in the world as liberator of the oppressed. Disagreeing with Cone, Charles Long contends that blackness is an "opaque" symbol, by which he means that blackness is a referent to the concrete historical and social reality which has influenced African American thought and consciousness.

---

54. Theophus H. Smith, "A Phenomenological Note: Black Religion as Christian Conjuration," *Journal of the Interdenominational Theological Center* 11 (fall 1983–spring 1984): 1.

55. Mitchell, "The Theological Posits of Black Christianity," in *Black Theology II*, ed. Bruce and Jones, 120.

According to Charles Long, blackness has its own distinct history and internal logic.[56] He claims that he is able to identify three basic components of blackness: (1) utopian thought, (2) alienation, and (3) the use of Western categories.[57] The tendency toward utopianism is reflected in black theology's "seeking a proper place, place here including also land where the Black will not be alien."[58] For African Americans lacking a sense of connection to land and institutions in the United States, they either long for Africa or relish a glorious African past, according to Charles Long. African Americans' feeling of alienation stems from their awareness that their presence in the United States is involuntary in that the vast majority of Africans entered the Western Hemisphere through forced slavery. In Long's opinion, because Africans in the New World lacked a common culture and language for communication, they used the culture and language of their enslavers to express themselves. He says, for instance,

> biblical imagery was used because it was at hand; it was adapted to and invested with the experience of the slave. Strangely enough, it was the slave who gave a religious meaning to the notions of freedom and land. The deliverance of the Children of Israel from the Egyptians became an archetype which enabled the slave to live with promise [of something better than slavery].[59]

In brief, these African slaves used Western categories such as biblical motifs, metaphors, eschatology, and so forth in Christianity, for the expression of thought clearly not in conformity with the mainstream of American thought.

While blackness is not in any way normative, scholars of American religion must recognize its history, structure, logic, and influence for two reasons, according to Long. First of all, blackness is a construct of American society, part and parcel to the nature and history of race relations in the United States. Second, blackness is an arena of experience and creativity not known to all Americans. Charles Long contends that

56. Charles H. Long, "Structural Similarities and Dissimilarities in Black and African Theologies," *Journal of Religious Thought* 33, no. 2 (fall–winter 1975): 21.
57. Ibid., 9–17.
58. Ibid., 12.
59. Long, *Significations,* 179.

W. E. B. DuBois rightly described the Black man in America as the possessor of a double consciousness and the same may be said to be true for all colonized peoples. He is a Black person living in a white world. His blackness is a source of otherness that not all Americans know or understand.[60]

Blackness is a reality with which African Americans are all too familiar and whites are not. However, as Long sees it, blackness does not exhaust fully nor reveal the whole identity of African Americans. Blackness is a form of otherness to African Americans as well as to their white counterparts. Blackness conceals from whites the harsh, unpleasant realities and less than ideal quality of the American way of life. Barred from full participation in American society and intellectual life, African Americans have chosen to explore and create meanings from this experience of otherness which is not known or understood by all Americans.[61] If Charles Long is right, no scholar can afford to ignore the influence of blackness on African American life and thought, not to mention the distortion and lack of critical self-awareness blackness creates among white Americans.

Just as the phenomenological approach does not privilege blackness, neither does that approach privilege liberation. Theophus Smith acknowledges the interest in liberation present in African American religion, but he does not think that African American religion is reducible to the experience of oppression and the desire to overcome it. He says,

> liberation theology as a discipline systematically abstracts and privileges selected contexts of liberation and oppression over against other forms of experience. In particular it subordinates traditions of spirituality that . . . also compel attention and empower social transformation. Earlier critics too have charged that black liberation theology so privileges the experience of oppression (its import and significance) that it tends to displace or supplant people's multifaceted religious experience with its one-dimensional interest in a hermeneutic of liberation. Black religious experience, however, is not reducible to the experience of

---

60. Long, "Structural Similarities and Dissimilarities in Black and African Theologies," 20.
61. Ibid., 21.

suffering and oppression, nor to the quest to overcome suffering and oppression.[62]

The earlier critics that Smith has in mind are Calvin E. Bruce, Carlton Lee, and Talbert Shaw. He goes on to say, "Liberationism is too specific an interest to encompass the full range of life trajectories of a people, even a severely oppressed people."[63]

Operating principally as a sociologist, C. Eric Lincoln is committed to a phenomenological approach. He says,

> the sociologist cannot tell you anything about souls, or ghosts, or demons, for example, because he has no equipment with which he can establish sensory contact with such phenomena, if indeed they do exist. . . . [T]he sociologist is prepared to observe, report, and interpret *what people do who assume the meaningful existence of phenomena which may or may not be available to scientific observation and measurement.*[64]

The sociologist can state the beliefs of a people but is in no position to say, through methodology, that these beliefs are right or wrong. Still, the sociologist can assess whether the beliefs are functional or dysfunctional with respect to the professed values of the group. As a committed sociologist also, Cheryl Gilkes would agree with Lincoln.

C. Eric Lincoln does not utilize the phenomenological method to privilege liberation; it already has privilege. By observation, not by any speculation or argumentation, liberation is of utmost importance to African Americans, according to Lincoln. Because liberation has this degree of importance, the sociologist of religion is obliged to address the issue of how well or poorly African American churches pursue liberation.

Lincoln does not consider blackness to be normative, although it is highly relevant to academic study for a number of reasons. First, while nonblacks can study religion adequately, the scholar's identification and participation in black cultural life may illuminate aspects of study that strict adherence to methodology alone cannot comprehend.[65] Second, and probably the most important reason, race is an aspect of African

---

62. Smith, *Conjuring Culture*, 178.
63. Ibid.
64. Lincoln, "Contemporary Black Religion," 93.
65. Ibid., 94–95.

American life, influencing African Americans' perceptions of reality, life chances, and so on. Third, change in conceptions of racial identity reflect change in a people's values.

For example, the change from "negro" to "black" marks a change in racial consciousness and values, according to Lincoln. The new concept of blackness that emerged in the 1960s involves: (1) a rejection of the previous concept of Negro and its associated norms; (2) a rejection of or opposition to "whiteness" and corresponding desire to be different, an insistence on racial pluralism; and (3) renewed commitment to freedom (liberation).[66] Lincoln explores the significance of race and the concept of blackness in *My Face Is Black* (1964), *Race, Religion, and the Continuing American Dilemma* (1984), and *Coming through the Fire: Surviving Race and Place in America* (1996).

For Cheryl Gilkes, too, blackness is not normative, but it is relevant to scholarship. She self-consciously identifies herself as a sociologist, not as a theologian or ethicist.[67] As a sociologist, she is committed to a phenomenological approach to religion; however, she believes that womanism may illuminate her teaching, research, and advocacy.[68] She points to three positive outcomes from her adoption of womanism. First, womanism provides her with a "way of reading and hearing."[69] Womanism suggests what she should look and listen for, and is what draws her to study a group of people and tap into a body of literature and tradition of oral history. Second, womanism recognizes diversity but emphasizes wholeness.[70] The womanist ideal recognizes that African American women are radically different from each other and that other patterns of diversity exist among African Americans. Still, the concept emphasizes that African Americans are one people and part of one larger human community. Third, womanism encourages interdisciplinary study and dialogue.[71] The concept defines interests and issues around which persons may communicate and cooperate with each other.

---

66. Lincoln, *The Black Church since Frazier,* 105–10. For a description of the rise and basic tenets of Negro racial identity, see Laurie F. Maffly-Kipp, "Mapping the World, Mapping the Race: Negro Race History, 1874–1915," *Church History* 64 (December 1995): 610–26.
67. Cheryl Townsend Gilkes, "Womanist Ideals and the Sociological Imagination," *Journal of Feminist Studies in Religion* 8, no. 2 (fall 1992): 147.
68. Ibid., 148.
69. Ibid., 149.
70. Ibid.
71. Ibid., 151.

An eschatological vision rather than phenomenology appears to be the norm that guides Charles Rooks's views on the place of race and liberation in black theology. He writes,

> The community of scholars I envision would certainly relate its intellectual inquiry to many folk: Africans and others in the Third World; the experiences of women, especially African American women; white university and seminary professors; political and economic movements in the U.S. and abroad; African American church people. The opportunities are immense. But the community must be defined fundamentally by a conviction and a commitment. The conviction: the African American religious experience has fundamental internal integrity that does not require external validation; the commitment: inquiry into and exploration of all possible dimensions of that important reality. The community thus would never define itself or be defined by interaction with or relation to other realities, including the long time oppressor of African America, white Western society.[72]

He thus envisions a community of scholars, in the future, that will come from various racial backgrounds and explore African American religion and culture from many perspectives, guided by a pursuit of truth more than racial rhetoric and ideology.

In addition to phenomenology, norms for the Human Sciences School appear to be drawn from prevailing academic canons of rationality and truth. The human sciences follow university criteria of scholarship. As human science disciplines, sociology, history of religions, and religious studies adhere also to canons of university scholarship.

## METHOD

In the Human Sciences School, methodology splinters into hermeneutics and science. On the one hand, Theophus Smith uses, as a hermeneutical methodology, the heuristic category of conjure for the study and interpretation of African American religion. He defines con-

---

72. Rooks, *Revolution in Zion*, 184.

jure as the practice of magic — seeking power and control over one's environment, using formula, imagery, and symbols and so forth found in the Bible.[73] Smith makes clear that African Americans are not the only group of persons who use magic. Non–African Americans in Western civilization also use conjure, and so he believes magic or conjure is a suitable category for the study of not only African American religion but the religion of other groups seeking empowerment.[74]

On the other hand, Henry Mitchell uses a more social scientific approach. Mitchell utilizes case study analysis for his description of core beliefs that African Americans hold. Over a ten-year period of research, Mitchell, along with Nicholas Cooper-Lewter, clinically documented and analyzed the beliefs that contributed to the mental stability of African Americans receiving pastoral counseling. As previously stated, those beliefs are belief in the providence, justice, majesty and omnipotence, omniscience, goodness, and grace of God; belief in the equality and uniqueness of all persons; belief that all persons are obliged to persevere in suffering; belief in the parenthood of God and the kinship of all peoples; and belief that life is good and worth living.

Charles Long argues that hermeneutics is the methodology that is most appropriate to the study of religion. According to Long, most studies of religion have inappropriately used the methodology of the social sciences.[75] Long is opposed to "scientism" in the study of religion. His rejection of scientism does not mean that he thinks that the study of religion is not a science. He believes that the study of a religion does constitute a science in the sense of having distinct data, methods, and discourse. He questions the applicability of scientism to the human sciences, which include religion. According to Long, the human sciences require their own methods and should not import or merely replicate the methods of the natural sciences. The religion of a people cannot be studied as a mere object alone, according to Long.[76] The people and the persons researching their religion must be viewed as participants in the same humanity. Long contends that hermeneutics, as a field of study that deals with and proposes solutions to the

---

73. Smith, *Conjuring Culture*, 4–6.
74. Ibid., 11.
75. Long, *Significations*, 173.
76. Ibid., 124.

problems of understanding, should inform all of the disciplines that make up the human sciences.[77]

Cheryl Gilkes and C. Eric Lincoln utilize both hermeneutics and, to a limited degree, social science methodology. Their use of hermeneutics is evident in their attention to description and analysis of religious practices. While their focus is on empirical phenomena, they do not subject all phenomena to systems of numerical measurement. For example, in *The Black Church in the African American Experience* (cowritten with Lawrence H. Mamiya), Lincoln uses both hermeneutics and social science methodology. He defines "black church" as black Christians with membership in predominately African American congregations. Next, he restricts the term to the major historically black denominations, where he estimates that 80 percent of black Christians are concentrated. After defining and narrowing application of the term, he constructs a "dialectical model," a set of six dichotomies that each allow for a wide range of data between extremes. The dichotomies are these: resistance/accommodation, priestly/prophetic, other-worldly/this-worldly, universalism/particularism, communal/privatistic, and charismatic/bureaucratic. He expects that significant differences will exist between churches and denominations on a variety of beliefs and practices. He uses surveys and questionnaires for collecting data. Once the data is collected, Lincoln analyzes and interprets what the results reveal about African American churches. His own experiences and observations, denominational histories, and previous academic studies of African American religion enrich his analysis.

## GOAL

For the Human Sciences School, the goal of black theology is knowledge for multiple purposes. Charles Rooks contends that the pursuit of knowledge must not be limited only to that knowledge leading to social action.[78] He insists that scholars giving thoughtful reflection on all kinds of issues affecting contemporary American society is proper. Moreover, scholars must discover all the dimensions of what being human means. Henry Mitchell rejects the notion that oppression has

---

77. Ibid., 91.
78. Rooks, *Revolution in Zion,* 137–39.

caused African Americans to focus more on food, drink, clothing, and other immediate needs for survival than on pondering the meaning of their lives as finite, created beings.[79]

As discussed earlier in the section on the tasks of black theology in the Human Sciences School, Charles Long describes the history of religions approach as the creation of structures — systematic presentations of a religion or religious meanings — to enable communications between persons and for them to explore and grasp anew what being human means while living under various situations. Rooks goes so far as to contend that all scholarly inquiry is of value, whether or not it has an immediate pragmatic use in the struggle for liberation. For Rooks, the pursuit of truth, wherever it leads, results in some positive consequence for human life.

Henry Mitchell seeks a kind of knowledge that has broad applications. He seeks knowledge that is relevant to both African Americans and non–African Americans. In describing the purposes of his study of core beliefs among African Americans, he writes:

> The purposes here are: (1) to retrieve and preserve the rich, life-giving affirmations of the Black oral tradition, and (2) to clinically validate and offer a pattern of belief and life that heals minds and spirits, helping to prevent personal and family disintegration. This practical, street-wise Soul culture has been seriously recorded and studied for its value as a spiritual survival source. It has been traced in individual case studies to explore how helpful Soul affirmations have been and can be in the healing of persons of all classes and ethnic groups.[80]

His use of the word "Soul" is synonymous with the phrase "African American core beliefs." While Mitchell finds retrieving, preserving and assessing African American core beliefs important, he asserts that these affirmations are significant to persons in any culture.[81] He sees as the desired end of his study an offering to "the world at large a set of

---

79. Mitchell and Cooper-Lewter, "The Theological Posits of Black Christianity," in *Black Theology II*, ed. Bruce and Jones, 116.

80. Mitchell, *Soul Theology*, x.

81. Ibid., 11.

road-tested posits for an existence in a society the massiveness and complexity of which dehumanizes whites as well as blacks."[82]

Though Henry Mitchell does not seek knowledge exclusively for use in liberation, he is still interested in useful knowledge. He not only wants to make persons aware of African American core beliefs but also he wants to strengthen these beliefs. According to him, the black theologian must construct theologies that enrich and further refine African American core beliefs.[83]

In a manner similar to Henry Mitchell, Theophus Smith is committed to the pursuit of knowledge both for the enrichment of African American religious beliefs and for increased understanding of all persons about these beliefs. Smith describes his concept of "conjure" as "a new conceptual paradigm for understanding Western religious and cultural phenomena."[84] For Smith, conjure is a concept of relevance to other groups of people in Western civilization who engage in magical practices using biblical imagery. Besides becoming more knowledgeable about conjure, his goal is "to advance — even correct and refine — [the Bible's] prescriptive efficacy for future conjurational performances."[85] In other words, the knowledge gained in his study is to be used to improve the use of the Bible in conjure or magical practices.

The emphasis of thinkers in the Human Sciences School on knowledge as the goal of academic black theology should not be mistaken as a total disinterest in the economic, social, and political problems that African Americans face. James Cone portrays the Society for the Study of Black Religion as an organization of scholars with little concern for the plight of African American communities. He writes,

> "Scholarship for the sake of scholarship" seemed to define most SSBR activity, and some of its members wondered how such an approach differed from white scholarship. As I saw the issue then and now (although not so clearly then), the problem of the second stage [of black theology in the SSBR] was not the academic focus of black theology, but rather the *accountability* of black theologians: for *what purpose,* and for *whom,* did they do

---

82. Mitchell, "The Theological Posits of Black Christianity," in *Black Theology II,* ed. Bruce and Jones, 120–21.

83. Ibid., 117–18.

84. Smith, *Conjuring Culture,* 11.

85. Ibid., 4.

theology? We did not explore these questions in sufficient depth and with adequate care.[86]

Charles Rooks agrees with James Cone that significant numbers of SSBR members were committed to the ideal of "scholarship for scholarship's sake." However, he differs with Cone in that he does not see the issue as lack of accountability. Instead, the issue is lack of recognizing the relevance and multiple purposes of scholarship.

Charles Rooks says that he, unlike James Cone, "was always certain the intellectual engagement of African-American seminary teachers would have an inevitable impact upon the education of future ordained church leaders."[87] His confidence is not altogether unfounded. The SSBR's relevance is demonstrated in its commitment to five tasks:

(1) the discovery and reclamation of an African American heritage that has been lost, unrecognized, or ignored as an entity of little or no value; (2) the development of a sense of dignity, worth, and pride in the African American heritage on the part of African American people; (3) the increase of knowledge and the development of skills that free African American people from oppression and dehumanization and enable them to survive in an unjust society; (4) the dissemination of information to persons of African American descent; and (5) the investigation and analysis of the African American religious experience.[88]

As Rooks understands the commitment of the SSBR to these tasks, the scholar is not obliged to focus solely on liberation. For him, not every single inquiry must be liberation-oriented. Taken as a whole though, he believes that all inquires contribute to the improvement of African American churches and communities. Truth is never a vain pursuit. He maintains therefore that "the true accountability, or obligation, of any scholar, African American or white, is always to the pursuit of truth, wherever it leads. No accountability to persons or organizations dictates or intrudes upon that quest."[89]

---

86. Cone, *For My People*, 26.
87. Rooks, *Revolution in Zion*, 138.
88. "Society for the Study of Black Religion," *Directory of African American Religious Bodies: A Compendium by the Howard University School of Divinity*, ed. Wardell J. Payne (Washington, D.C.: Howard University Press, 1991), 177.
89. Rooks, *Revolution in Zion*, 138.

Charles Rooks is not opposed to social activism. He just happens to think that it lies outside of academic study and is an entirely separate arena. One reason for his being adamant about keeping the SSBR focused on academic concerns during his presidency of the organization was his belief that many arenas exist for social and political action but few for research, reflection, and dialogue among African American scholars. The activities that he, more than likely, considered proper to the SSBR were "(1) [providing] an intellectual forum for African Americans in religion; (2) [stimulating] African American religious scholarship and research; and (3) [providing] fellowship for African American scholars and teachers in religion."[90] The event highlighting these activities may be the annual meeting of the SSBR, where members read papers and discuss their views in trends and issues in African American religions. In Rooks's thinking, this kind of scholarly activity within the SSBR is important but may not seem as such to persons who are confused about the calling to scholarship as it relates to African American churches and communities.

As president of the SSBR, Charles Rooks stressed that "African American churches are indispensable in determining the life and culture of African America."[91] He says truly, "There is still no other institution in African America's life that daily reaches as many people as churches."[92] Unfortunately, these churches do not have and are therefore in dire need of an adequate supply of clergy with formal training, according to Rooks.[93] This dilemma poses the question: "Who will teach and what will they teach clergy preparing for and committed to service in African American churches?" Rooks finds an answer to this question in the recruitment and financial support of African Americans in graduate theological education for research and teaching and their eventual placement in professorships. For him, the existence and growth of a scholarly community committed to the study of all possible dimensions of African American religion is crucial to the education of African American clergy.[94]

---

90. "Society for the Study of Black Religion," *Directory of African American Religious Bodies,* ed. Wardell J. Payne, 177.
91. Rooks, *Revolution in Zion,* 186.
92. Ibid., 187.
93. Ibid., 189.
94. Ibid., 184.

Cheryl Gilkes and C. Eric Lincoln, through inquiry, seek knowledge for not only greater understanding but also the improvement of American society in general, and African American churches and communities in particular. Lincoln says that the black church is the "cultural womb" of the African American community and, as a result, has given rise and support to other black institutions and movements. Any significant change in black cultural life must spread from African American churches. With this perspective in view, through her research, Gilkes has discovered areas requiring immediate attention: for example, (1) disparity between genders (i.e., the oppression and suppression of women), (2) poverty and other misfortunes (e.g., unemployment, inadequate education, crime, family deterioration, etc.) related to or stemming from poverty, (3) lack of social responsibility among middle-class blacks, and (4) deficiency in clergy education and underutilization of professionally trained persons in African American churches.[95]

Based on Lincoln's study of African American churches, he identifies as areas of concern (1) education and training for clergy; (2) conjoining with salary, benefits for clergy, such as housing allowance, health insurance, and pension; (3) increasing clergy supply and removing restrictions on women in ordained ministry; and (4) support and nurture for families.[96] With respect to academic black theology, he recommends (1) that black theologians give more attention to the hermeneutical traditions (how persons actually structure and explain their experiences) within African American communities and (2) that black theologians utilize mass and popular media of communication and informal systems of black clergy education for disseminating their ideas.[97] The fruits of black theological research have yet to find their way to the majority of black Christians, clergy or laity, according to Lincoln.[98]

## SUMMARY

Using the works of Cheryl Gilkes, C. Eric Lincoln, Charles Long, Henry Mitchell, Charles Rooks, and Theophus Smith, this chapter

---

95. Cheryl Townsend Gilkes, "Plenty Good Room: Adaptation in a Changing Black Church," *Annals of the American Academy of Political and Social Science* 558 (July 1998): 101–17.

96. Lincoln and Mamiya, *The Black Church in the African American Experience,* 399–404.

97. Ibid., 181.

98. Ibid, 169 (Chart I), 178–82.

defines the methodological perspective of the Human Sciences School on the tasks, content, sources, norm, method, and goal of academic black theology.

The tasks of theology are description, analysis, evaluation, explanation, and revision. Charles Long prefers to call the task of revision "deconstruction." He and Henry Mitchell are suspicious of the task of construction, if it is characterized by imaginative invention. They accept systematic construction in black theology when it is done inductively, that is, when it is based upon thorough empirical description of the beliefs and practices that actually exist in a community of people.

The content or theme of black theology is empowerment. Thinkers in the Human Sciences School, namely, Long, Mitchell, and Smith, emphasize how religion empowers and sustains African Americans in the face of life's difficulties, not only in situations of oppression but also in times of loneliness, bereavement, divorce, sickness, and any other experiences that make life hard to endure. Lincoln does not deny that African American religion has multiple themes. He claims that liberation is its principal theme.

The principal source is African American or black religion. Long defines religion as a complex cultural phenomenon that involves various experiences, expressions, motivations, intentions, behaviors, styles, rhythms, and structures of thought, beliefs, and traditions that are not restricted to Christianity or any other overt form of organized religion. As a complex system, African American religion does not exist in a vacuum. It has no absolute, unique black essence and is influenced by and influences other religions and trends in American society. For the study and interpretation of African American religion, Smith and Mitchell, between the two of them, utilize sources such as clinical psychology, ethnomusicology, biblical hermeneutics, phenomenology, and literary criticism.

Phenomenological conceptions of religion are normative for the Human Sciences School. The phenomenological approach is a program of study that is compatible with the academic study of religion according to prevailing university canons of rationality and truth. Within the Human Sciences School, African American religion is supposedly studied for how it operates and is understood in the lives of its adherents. According to Mitchell, African American religion is distinguished by its function of giving persons psychological and spiritual wholeness. According to Smith, African American religion functions to give people imagined or real power over conditions in their lives. Long sees religion as enabling persons to overcome the hardness of life.

The phenomenological approach and its aim of objectivity in the study of religion accords no special authority to blackness. Blackness is seen only as a historical and social construct that has influenced American life. Long contends that blackness has its own history and logic and does not fully exhaust African American identity and culture. However, he thinks that scholars cannot afford to ignore its influence on African American life and thought and the distortion and lack of critical self-awareness it creates among white Americans who are often oblivious to the harsh, unpleasant realities of the American way of life.

Phenomenology is not the norm that guides Charles Rooks. He is guided by an eschatological vision. He envisions a future community of scholars who will come from various racial backgrounds and explore African American religion and culture from many perspectives.

Just as the phenomenological approach does not privilege blackness, neither does that approach privilege liberation. Smith acknowledges the interest in liberation that is present in African American religion, but he does not think that African American religion is reducible to the experience of oppression and the desire to overcome it. He contends that African American religion, like any other religion, is multifaceted. Lincoln does not deny this viewpoint. But his application of the phenomenological approach leads him to acknowledge, as a matter of fact, that liberation is the principal concern of African Americans.

Method in the Human Sciences School splinters into hermeneutics and science. Long argues that the appropriate method is hermeneutics. Smith utilizes the hermeneutical method of heuristic categories for explanation. Mitchell uses case study analysis. Lincoln uses both hermeneutics and social science methodology.

The goal of the Human Sciences School is knowledge for multiple purposes. For example, Mitchell's aim is to identify and describe core beliefs that enable sound mental health. Smith's aim is to understand and improve conjure, the use of biblical formulae for gaining power. Gilkes and Lincoln, through their research, identify the scope and magnitude of problems requiring the immediate attention and action of African American churches and communities. Rooks contends that knowledge has intrinsic value and therefore does not have to be serviceable to black liberation in order to have value, yet Rooks is not disinterested in liberation. He claims that social activism must be pursued in arenas outside of academic study. For him, within the academic arena, scholarship must be for scholarship's sake — that is, for the unencumbered pursuit of knowledge. However, Rooks contends that, as a whole, all scholarly inquiries contribute to the improvement of African American churches and communities. For Rooks, the key to progressive social action in African American churches and communities requires a scholarly community committed to the study of African American religion, from all possible dimensions, and the education of clergy for service in these churches, which make up the one major institution that touches the lives of nearly all African Americans.

# CHAPTER FIVE

# An Assessment and Future Directions of Black Theology

**A**FTER EXAMINING the Black Hermeneutical, the Black Philosophical, and the Human Sciences schools of black theology, we can draw several conclusions. In this final chapter, I want to emphasize only three. After outlining these conclusions, I summarize points of similarity and difference among the three schools as a means of suggesting future directions for African American theology.

First, we may conclude from this study that academic black theology is not the sole bearer of the African American theological tradition. Black theology is not constituted by nor does it depend on the activities of professional systematic theologians for its existence and development. Chapter 1 shows that the black oral tradition is the principal bearer of black theology. None of the leading intellectuals in the oral tradition are professional systematic theologians.

As I mentioned in chapter 1, Gayraud Wilmore's and J. Deotis Roberts's distinction between formal and informal black theology, and other black theologians' dramatization of the rivalry between themselves and black church leaders obfuscate the relation of black theology in academic settings with its oral transmission in African American churches and communities. Several black theologians are members of African American churches and very much involved in the affairs of their communities. Academic black theologians are putting into print the oral traditions to which they have been exposed, but many traditions need recognition, several of which still are to see print.

Second, several ways exist for doing black theology. The oral tradition in churches and communities represents one set of ways of doing black theology. The academic setting represents another set of ways of doing black theology. I have examined only the set of approaches

145

to black theology in academic settings. As this study shows, the three schools examined in chapters 2, 3, and 4 each represent a unique way of doing black theology. Doing academic black theology is not restricted to only one approach.

Third, the plurality of approaches to black theology makes the issue of public theology of vital concern. Communication within African American communities and between these communities and other groups of people is urgently needed. Professional academic theologians have no privileged position in debates or dialogue with African American church leaders. But neither do African American church leaders have authoritative status in academic black theology. Professional systematic theologians and church leaders must both communicate to persons outside of their settings.

## THE RELATIONSHIP OF BLACK THEOLOGY TO PUBLIC THEOLOGY

That academic black theologians will be heard is not a given; however, they do deserve to be heard. The sustained and very disciplined inquiries into black theology that professional academic theologians undertake can enrich conversations on and the practice of black theology in African American churches and communities. African American church and community leaders often lack critical methods for assessing the beliefs of their churches and communities. Black theology scholars must work hard to be heard and to have the relevance of their work recognized. They will have to attend to the five contexts of public theology that I mention later in this chapter. As I mentioned in chapter 4, C. Eric Lincoln stresses the contexts of use and study of the language of the church or community and publication, instruction, and discussion in existing forums or media that reach the masses of African Americans where they are in the churches and communities.

William R. Jones's *Is God a White Racist?* is a highly sophisticated and thought-provoking book. He attempts to show that leading black theologians — namely, James Cone, Albert Cleage, Joseph Washington, Major Jones, and J. Deotis Roberts — lack sufficient foundations for their theological programs. According to Jones, these leading theologians' black liberation theism — the belief that God is in solidarity with and thus working to liberate oppressed black people —

is untenable in the absence of empirical evidence that demonstrates unambiguously God's solidarity with oppressed blacks.

James Cone's comment about Jones's book is most revealing. He writes,

> [it] remains as a challenge to Black theological proposals and will continue to require the serious attention of Black theologians. We cannot remain satisfied with an easy internal solution, because what we say about God and suffering should be publicly defensible outside the confessional contexts from which they emerge. If we do not test the credibility of our theological judgments in a public arena, without resource to confessional narrowness, then we should not complain if what we say about God is ignored by those outside of our confession of faith. It is because Christians claim to have a universal message that they are required to speak its truth in a language publicly accessible to all.[1]

To Jones's demand for evidence justifying belief in black liberation theism, Cone cites the ministry, death, and resurrection of Jesus Christ as the definitive proof of God's solidarity with the oppressed and therefore with black people because they have experienced oppression.[2] However, he recognizes the implications of Jones's claims that academic black theology, as practiced by himself and the vast majority of black theologians, is irrelevant to an intelligent public.

Black theology must become "public theology." Theology that is public involves: (1) the use of faith, theological language, and other religious resources in the resolution of societal and cultural problems; (2) interaction with — that is, scrutinizing and interpreting — the actual beliefs and practices of a religious community; (3) the use of prevalent standards of truth, rationality, and argument; (4) dialogue and collaboration with persons outside the theologian's circle and community of faith, academic specialty, and social class; and (5) in addition to traditional means of publishing academic study, the use of popular media such as television, radio, newspaper, church learning institutes, fiction, poetry, film, and so forth for disseminating knowledge.

---

1. Cone, "An Interpretation of the Debate among Black Theologians," Epilogue to *Black Theology: A Documentary History, 1966–1979*, ed. Cone and Wilmore, 621–22.
2. Ibid., 621; idem, *God of the Oppressed*, 191–92.

Each meaning of public theology must find expression and receive emphasis in the field of black theology. Jones is mistaken if he holds to the view that epistemic publicity is evident only from his perspective. The Black Hermeneutical and Human Sciences schools as well as the Black Philosophical School are epistemically public. Each school has its own unique approach and capabilities for making black theology intellectually and publicly accessible. Presently, however, the need exists for demonstrating publicness of black theology in terms of its openness to multiple interpretations of African American religion and culture, using prevalent standards of rationality in the university, conducting black theological research within a climate of interdisciplinary and interracial dialogue and cooperation, and utilizing popular media for disseminating the fruits of black theological research.

## ANALYSIS OF BLACK THEOLOGICAL SCHOOLS

In chapters 2, 3, and 4, we identified and examined the Black Hermeneutical, Black Philosophical, and Human Sciences schools — the three schools of thought in contemporary academic black theology — in terms of how each school defines the tasks, sources, method, norms, content, and goal of black theology. As we learned, the earliest shared methodological perspective among black theologians was first identified by Charles B. Copher, who observed that various thinkers' views on the Bible were part of a single quest for a "black hermeneutic" — a method of biblical interpretation that retrieves and is representationally accurate to the earliest expressions of Christian faith among African Americans in the United States. For this reason, this earliest detected perspective may be called the Black Hermeneutical School. The entry of philosophers of religion into and the use of philosophy in the field of academic black theology resulted in the formation of the Black Philosophical School. The Human Sciences School was formed upon the entry of historians of religion, theologians of culture, sociologists of religion, and other scholars committed to the academic study of black religion as a cultural phenomenon in human life into the field of academic black theology.

All schools accept description, analysis, evaluation, explanation, and revision as tasks of black theology. The task of construction is accepted in the Black Hermeneutical and Black Philosophical schools.

In the Human Sciences School, however, construction may be either rejected if it is understood to mean imaginative invention, as it is by Charles Long and Henry Mitchell, or accepted if it means an inductive approach to structuring the beliefs in a religion that have been identified through empirical analysis or phenomenological description. James Evans, in the Black Hermeneutical School, and Charles Long, in the Human Sciences School, both prefer to call the task of revision "deconstruction." In the Black Philosophical School, William R. Jones prefers to call the task of revision "gnosiological conversion."

The Black Hermeneutical and the Black Philosophical schools both affirm liberation as the content of black theology. Whereas the Black Hermeneutical School defines liberation in terms of biblical conceptions of God's liberating activity and black folk stories on freedom, the Black Philosophical School defines liberation in terms of social and political philosophy, which may or may not be compatible with biblical story and black story. In the Black Hermeneutical School, liberation is related to other themes found in the Bible such as reconciliation (J. Deotis Roberts), hope (Major Jones), redemption (Olin Moyd), and survival (Delores Williams). In the Black Philosophical School, liberation means a vision of life with possibilities for fulfillment (Anthony Pinn), the overthrow of capitalism (Cornel West), cultural pluralism (Henry Young), and anything recommended by accurate description of a people's situation (William R. Jones).

For the Human Sciences School, empowerment is the content of black theology. Thinkers in the Human Sciences School emphasize the capacity of religion to empower and sustain persons in a variety of difficult or stressful situations in life, which not only includes oppression but also loneliness, divorce, bereavement, sickness, and so forth. Olin Moyd's concept of redemption bears much similarity to the notion of empowerment in the Human Sciences School. C. Eric Lincoln accepts the existence of multiple themes in African American religion but insists, as matter of fact, that liberation is the principal theme of interest to African Americans. He defines liberation as the restoration of human dignity and the negation of violence (verbal, mental, physical, social, etc.)

All schools accept the black experience as a source of black theology. Across the three schools, Katie Cannon, Kelly Douglas, Cheryl Gilkes, Jacquelyn Grant, Alice Walker, and Delores Williams emphasize the use of women's experience. For the Black Hermeneutical School, the principal source of black theology is revelation, which is complemented by the Bible, tradition, black experience, history, spirituality, and culture, as well as reason when it is compatible with revelation. For the Black Philosophical School, reason in the form of philosophy is the principal source of black theology, followed by the black experience in all of its multiple dimensions. The Human Sciences School focuses on African American religion and culture, which it understands as a complex phenomenon that involves various experiences, expressions, motivations, intentions, behaviors, styles, rhythms, structures of thought, beliefs, and traditions that are not restricted to Christianity or any other overt form of religion.

The Black Hermeneutical, Black Philosophical, and Human Sciences schools differ on what they consider the norm of black theology. The Black Hermeneutical School derives its criteria of truth from non-foundationalist (e.g., biblical, communal, and personal) conceptions of Christian faith. These beliefs revolve around the central affirmation that Jesus Christ is black. The blackness of Christ may be understood to be either historical/physical (Albert Cleage), ontological (James Cone, Jacquelyn Grant, and Kelly Douglas), mythological (J. Deotis Roberts), or pneumatological (Dwight Hopkins). However expressed, the blackness of Christ leads to three other beliefs that have normative quality in the Black Hermeneutical School: (1) the belief that God is black, that is, in solidarity with oppressed African Americans and will liberate them; (2) the belief that liberation, as an activity of God, is of infinite and unquestionable value; and (3) the belief that the black experience is *heilsgeschichte,* a part of sacred history, and therefore cannot be ignored or minimized in theological reflection.

The norms of the Black Philosophical and Human Sciences schools are foundationalist conceptions of religion. On the one hand, the Black Philosophical School grounds its understanding of Christian faith in humanistic thought. William R. Jones, Henry Young, and Cornel West, as weak humanists, in various ways modify and/or affirm Christian faith in order to maintain emphasis on human freedom. Each espouses a variant of what William R. Jones calls "humanocentric theism." Alice Walker subscribes also to a weak version of humanism. She, however, affirms belief in a pantheistic spirituality that is compatible, at several points, with Jones's description of humanocentric theism. As a strong humanist, Anthony Pinn subscribes to atheism and denies altogether the authority of Christian faith in academic scholarship and black liberation. Thinkers in the Black Philosophical School do not privilege the black experience, but they do privilege liberation. They emphasize African Americans' membership in the human race, not above it or below it, and the desirability of liberation because, apart from God's will, oppressed people want it. On the other hand, the Human Sciences School grounds its understanding of religion in phenomenology. African American religion is studied for the ways it operates and is understood in the lives of its adherents.

The phenomenological approach accords no special authority to blackness or liberation. Charles Long contends that blackness is a historical and social construct that has influenced American life but does not exhaust or fully capture the whole of African American identity and experience. For C. Eric Lincoln too, blackness is not normative but is an aspect of American life that the scholar cannot afford to ignore. Still committed to the phenomenological approach, Lincoln claims that blackness and Cheryl Gilkes claims that womanism, though neither is a prerequisite for studying African American religion and culture, may illuminate the scholar's work where methodology alone does not. Theophus Smith contends that liberation does not encompass all expressions of African American religion. He maintains that religion, even of oppressed people, is multifaceted. Lincoln does not deny this approach but he maintains that liberation, as matter of fact, is of utmost importance to African Americans. Charles Rooks's eschatological vision is compatible with the phenomenological approach that does not privilege blackness or liberation. Both the Black Philosophical and Human Sciences schools accept prevailing academic canons of truth and rationality in each one's assessment of theological claims. In addition to academic canons, thinkers in the Black Philosophical School assess theological claims in terms of the logical constraints of their chosen systems of philosophy. Theologians in the Black Hermeneutical School, such as James Cone and James Evans, contend that black Christian faith has its own logic and is not obliged to follow prevailing canons of rationality in order to be intelligible.

The three schools differ on the method of black theology. As implied in its name, the Black Hermeneutical School makes hermeneutics the method of black theology. Specific hermeneutical methods used in the

Black Hermeneutical School are biblical hermeneutics, correlation, narrative criticism, and philosophical hermeneutics. The philosophically oriented methodology of the Black Philosophical School encompasses specific methods such as philosophical analysis, logical argument, and philosophical and biblical hermeneutics. The methodology of the Human Sciences School divides between hermeneutics and social sciences methodologies.

The three schools of academic black theology also differ on the goal of black theology. Both the Black Hermeneutical and Black Philosophical schools declare that moral and ethical action leading to liberation is the goal of black theology. Through eschatology and virtue theory based on the lives of exemplary individuals in the black liberation struggle, black theologians in the Black Hermeneutical School develop guides for moral and ethical action. In the Black Philosophical School, Jones contends that liberation is contextual; its form and means depend upon the situation of an oppressed people. For him, liberating action becomes obvious only after an accurate diagnosis of a situation of injustice. Alice Walker underscores the role of personal choice in determining appropriate, socially responsible action. In contrast to these schools, the Human Sciences School declares that knowledge, which may serve multiple purposes, is the goal of black theology.

Notwithstanding these differences, each school recognizes African American churches as the major institution for black liberation and emphasizes the need of reform in these churches in order for them to truly function as a base for liberation. African American churches are the core institution in African American communities over which African Americans have ownership and control. In C. Eric Lincoln's study of African American churches, he infers that 86 percent of African American Christians holds membership in historic, predominately black Christian churches. In the Black Philosophical School, Cornel West contends, however, that these churches alone cannot do the work of liberation. They must work in conjunction with other institutions to achieve change in American society. In the Black Hermeneutical School, James Cone is not opposed to the idea of coalitions between African American churches and other institutions. He insists that internal reforms and black solidarity must precede coalition-building. In the Human Sciences School, Charles Rooks emphasizes the need for reform in theological education. He is committed to the ideal of scholarship for scholarship's sake but considers this ideal relevant to the task of strengthening African American churches for ministry and social action. The overwhelming majority of African American clergy lack any formal training. They are in need of knowledge and skills in ministry, according to Rooks. For him, the solution to this dilemma is a scholarly community committed to the study of African American religion and the education of African American clergy.

The Black Hermeneutical School has been and continues to be the most prolific and popular of the three schools of academic black theology. The Black Hermeneutical School may owe its widespread appeal to its "familiarity" to persons uninitiated into the field of academic black theology. Delores Williams notes the appreciation of her students, at all seminaries where she has taught, for James Cone's simple and nonpretentious theological language.[3] All thinkers in the Black Hermeneutical School who have entered dialogue with Cone share his nonconvoluted use of language. Thinkers in the Black Hermeneutical School tend to use symbols and styles of reasoning familiar to persons uninitiated in their academic discipline. The philosophical and scientific barriers — for example, in the works of thinkers such as William R. Jones and Theophus Smith — pose great difficulties for persons uninitiated in the literature and methods of philosophy and the human and social sciences. Reading and comprehension of works in the Black Philosophical and Human Sciences schools requires a background of study in or prior exposure to those schools' philosophies and scientific methodologies.

Literary production, popular appeal, and simplicity of language are not the only or the most reliable measures of the academic potential of each school. Though the smallest and least prolific, the Human Sciences School has admirable qualities. First of all, the Human Sciences School is open to the use of themes and categories broader than the theme of liberation, presently the sole focus of the Black Hermeneutical and Black Philosophical schools. In the Human Sciences School, the theme of empowerment is broad enough to include not

---

3. Delores S. Williams, "James Cone's Liberation: Twenty Years Later," in *A Black Theology of Liberation*, Twentieth Anniversary Edition, 194–95.

only interest in overcoming oppression but also any other situations in human life that are of concern to human beings seeking fulfillment. Olin Moyd's conception of redemption is compatible with the notion of empowerment in the Human Sciences School. Second, scholarship in the Human Sciences School does not have the burden of showing itself politically useful, as in the case of the Black Hermeneutical and Black Philosophical schools. Studies that do not have any obvious connection to liberation are regarded as valuable in the Human Sciences School, whereas they are not so regarded in the Black Hermeneutical and Black Philosophical schools. Third, the Human Sciences School defines African American religion broadly, making possible comparative studies between it and other religions and non–African American peoples. For example, Charles Long and Henry Mitchell contend that African American religion is not characterized by some absolute, unique black essence but can be studied in comparison to other religions and also in acknowledgment of the mutual influence between it and other religions. Theophus Smith insists that his concept of conjure — the performance of magic using the Bible — is applicable not only to African Americans but to many groups of people in Western civilization.

## AREAS OF DEVELOPMENT FOR AFRICAN AMERICAN THEOLOGY

I end now by pointing to those areas of new or continuing development in African American theology: (1) liberation theology, (2) treatment of multiple themes in African American religion and culture, (3) increasing research and publication from the Black Philosophical and Human Sciences schools, (4) womanist theology, (5) Catholic Christian theology from African American perspectives and theological studies of non-Christian religions and secular intellectual traditions, (6) cultural pluralist conceptions of racial identity and social justice, and (7) linguistic studies.

Though African American theology is not synonymous with liberation theology, overcoming economic, social, and political oppression will remain a matter of ultimate concern for African Americans. The fact is saddening but true that racial and social inequality does exist in the United States. Conscientious persons from various religious and intellectual traditions in African American life and culture will continue to address this matter, as they have done in the past, with great passion for and commitment to achieving social justice. The Black Hermeneutical, Black Philosophical, and Human Sciences schools, and any other future methodological perspective will, in their own ways, address the problem of racial and social inequality in the myriad of forms it manifests itself.

The Black Hermeneutical, Black Philosophical, and Human Sciences schools are well established frameworks of interpretation and will continue to provide persons with bases for approaching the study of African American religion and culture. By no means underestimating the importance of liberation theology, all schools will begin to address themes in African American religion and culture other than liberation. The Human Sciences School already has an openness to multiple themes. Possibly the Black Philosophical and Black Hermeneutical schools will modify themselves somewhat in order to address multiple themes. Olin Moyd and Cheryl Sanders are already moving in that direction. While holding much in common with other thinkers in the Black Hermeneutical School, Moyd and Sanders have proposed the themes of redemption and empowerment respectively as conceptions that are inclusive of economic, social, and political concerns as well as personal, spiritual matters.

Though the Black Hermeneutical, Black Philosophical, and Human Sciences schools are well-established frameworks of interpretation that will continue to enrich the field of African American theology, increasing research and publication will be done from the perspectives of the Black Philosophical and Human Sciences schools. Persons seeking alternatives to the Black Hermeneutical School, the dominant tradition in contemporary black theology, may turn to the Black Philosophical and Human Sciences perspectives. This book provides a thorough description of these perspectives, something never before available, and establishes their legitimacy as viable methodological perspectives in the contemporary black theological movement.

Womanist theologians are still in the process of giving clarity and distinctiveness to their voices and perspectives in African American theology. More constructive and theoretical work can be expected in this area. Women have been historically underrepresented in the highest levels of church and community leadership as well as in the field of theological and religious studies. Work from the perspective of women's experiences and matters of concern for women will enrich the field of African American theology for many years to come. By womanist theology's giving voice to women, for so long held to silence, womanist theology will encourage other suppressed groups (i.e., gay and lesbian, youth, elderly, disabled, conservatives, etc.) within African American communities to make their voices heard in theological and religious studies.

Without question, evangelical Protestant Christianity is the predominant form of religious expression in the African American population, but other religious and intellectual traditions of historical quality and social significance exist in African American life and culture. The field of African American theology must, and will, expand to an examination, for example, of Roman Catholic and Orthodox Christianity, Islam, santeria, conjure, vodou, and eclectic spiritualist traditions.

The prevalent concept of racial identity in black theology, especially the Black Hermeneutical School, is contra-culturalist, where blackness is defined over against and in opposition to whiteness. Black racial identity and social change has been informed mostly by nationalism (a form of contra-culturalism) and integrationism (a form of monoculturalism that subordinates or devalues blackness in preference to whiteness). Another intellectual tradition of cultural pluralism exists that acknowledges and appreciates difference without extolling or devaluing any ethnic group. Victor Anderson's *Beyond Ontological Blackness* exposes the limitation of the contra-culturalist conception of racial identity in African American theology. As a matter of fact, he argues that this form of racial identity is logically incoherent. He proposes the use of alternative conceptions of blackness that presuppose a form of cultural pluralism that affirms all humans in the quest for fulfillment in life. According to Anderson, contemporary thinkers who are calling for this alternative conception of blackness include Cornel West, bell hooks, Toni Morrison, Alice Walker, Henry Louis Gates, Houston Baker, Darlene Clark Hine, Wilson Moses, Michael Dyson, and Joe Wood. These contemporary thinkers follow in the tradition of people like Howard Thurman, W. E. B. Du Bois, and Zora Neale Hurston, to name a few. Henry Young's *Hope in Process* proposes a framework for understanding cultural pluralism and encouraging action toward social justice. In the future, African American constructive theology will involve more and more correlation of religious beliefs with conceptions of race and society within this tradition of cultural pluralism.

A very important area of development is in linguistic studies. C. Eric Lincoln contends that descriptive studies of the oral traditions of black theology are crucial for the enrichment of African American theological study. Lincoln calls for a closer connection between academic study and the actual language and concepts that persons use in a religious community. In addition to grounding academic study in living religious communities, linguistic studies are important for the development of theological methodology. Gayraud Wilmore and J. Deotis Roberts have said that the development of a methodological perspective rooted in African American religious language is a daunting task and may be best left to future generations of scholars. The future is now upon us.

Important work in this area has already begun. For example, Will E. Coleman's *Tribal Talk* and Gerald L. Davis's *I Got the Word in Me* and his documentary film entitled "The Performed Word" are installments on the greater benefit to be reaped in theology through the study of metaphor, idioms, rules, logic, and modes of understanding in African American communication. These linguistic studies and others will provide bases for the construction of hermeneutics and methodological perspectives that are sensitive and relevant to the African American religious beliefs under examination, more so than the existing framework of black theology crafted from borrowings from white Western theologians named in the preface of this book.

In the future, African American theology, as an academic discipline, will gain a breadth of topics, themes, methods, and so forth greater than that exhibited in the first three decades of the contemporary black theological movement. African American theology will no longer be synonymous with liberation theology, womanist theology, or Christian theology. These specialized areas of inquiry will be seen more as distinct parts of the field rather than, as they have been before, paradigms or models for the entire field of study. African American theology will include study of all religious beliefs and intellectual traditions present in African American life and culture.

# Bibliography

Anderson, Victor. *Beyond Ontological Blackness: An Essay on African American Religious and Cultural Criticism.* New York: Continuum, 1995.

Baker-Fletcher, Karen, and Garth Kasimu Baker-Fletcher. *My Sister, My Brother: Womanist and Xodus God-Talk.* Maryknoll, N.Y.: Orbis Books, 1997.

Brotz, Howard. *The Black Jews of Harlem: Negro Nationalism and the Dilemmas of Negro Leadership.* New York: Schocken Books, 1970.

Bruce, Calvin E., and William R. Jones, eds. *Black Theology II: Essays on the Formation and Outreach of Contemporary Black Theology.* Lewisburg, Pa.: Bucknell University Press, 1978.

Cady, Lindell E. *Religion, Theology, and American Public Life.* Albany: State University of New York Press, 1993.

Cannon, Katie G. *Black Womanist Ethics.* Atlanta: Scholars Press, 1988.

———. *Katie's Canon: Womanism and the Soul of the Black Community.* New York: Continuum, 1995.

Chapman, Mark L. *Christianity on Trial: African-American Religious Thought before and after Black Power.* Maryknoll, N.Y.: Orbis Books, 1996.

Cleage, Albert B., Jr. *Black Christian Nationalism.* New York: William Morrow & Co., 1972.

———. *The Black Messiah.* New York: Sheed and Ward, 1968; reprinted, Trenton, N.J.: Africa World Press, 1989.

Coleman, Will E. *Tribal Talk: Black Theology, Hermeneutics, and African American Ways of "Telling the Story."* University Park: Pennsylvania State University Press, 2000.

Collins, Patricia Hill. *Black Feminist Thought: Knowledge, Consciousness, and the Politics of Empowerment.* Boston: Unwin Hyman, 1990.

Cone, Cecil W. *The Identity Crisis in Black Theology.* Nashville: African Methodist Episcopal Church, 1975.

Cone, James H. "Black Power, Black Theology, and the Study of Theology and Ethics." *Theological Education* 6 (spring 1970): 202–15.

———. *Black Theology and Black Power.* Twentieth Anniversary Edition. New York: Seabury Press, 1969; San Francisco: HarperCollins, 1989.

———. *A Black Theology of Liberation.* Twentieth Anniversary Edition. Philadelphia: Lippincott, 1970; Maryknoll, N.Y.: Orbis Books, 1990.

———. "Black Theology on Revolution, Violence, and Reconciliation." *Dialog* 12 (spring 1973): 127–33.

———. *For My People: Black Theology and the Black Church.* Maryknoll, N.Y.: Orbis Books, 1984.

———. "God Is Black." In *Lift Every Voice: Constructing Christian Theologies from the Underside,* ed. Susan Brooks Thistlethwaite and Mary Potter Engel, pp. 81–94. San Francisco: Harper & Row, 1990.

———. *God of the Oppressed.* San Francisco: Harper & Row, Seabury Press, 1975.

———. *God of the Oppressed.* Revised with new introduction. San Francisco: Harper & Row, Seabury Press, 1975; Maryknoll, N.Y.: Orbis Books, 1997.

———. "The Gospel and the Liberation of the Poor: How My Mind Has Changed." *Christian Century* 98 (February 18, 1981): 162–66.

———. "Looking Back, Going Forward: Black Theology as Public Theology." *Criterion* 38 (winter 1999): 18–27, 46.

———. *Martin and Malcolm and America: A Dream or a Nightmare?* Maryknoll, N.Y.: Orbis Books, 1991.

———. *My Soul Looks Back.* Nashville: Abingdon Press, 1982; Maryknoll, N.Y.: Orbis Books, 1986.

———. *Risks of Faith: The Emergence of a Black Theology of Liberation, 1968–1998.* Beacon Press, 1999.

———. *Speaking the Truth: Ecumenism, Liberation, and Black Theology.* Grand Rapids: Eerdmans, 1986.

———. *The Spirituals and the Blues: An Interpretation.* New York: Seabury Press, 1972; Maryknoll, N.Y.: Orbis Books, 1991.

———, and Gayraud S. Wilmore, eds. *Black Theology: A Documentary History, 1966–1979.* Maryknoll, N.Y.: Orbis Books, 1979.

———, and Gayraud S. Wilmore, eds. *Black Theology: A Documentary History, Volume Two: 1980–1992.* Maryknoll, N.Y.: Orbis Books, 1993.

Copher, Charles B. *Black Biblical Studies: An Anthology of Charles B. Copher: Biblical and Theological Issues on the Black Presence in the Bible.* Chicago: Black Light Fellowship, 1993.

Costen, James H. "Black Theological Education: Its Context, Content, and Conduct." *Journal of the Interdenominational Theological Center* 12 (fall 1984–spring 1985): 1–8.

Cummings, George C. L. *A Common Journey.* Maryknoll, N.Y.: Orbis Books, 1993.

———, and Dwight N. Hopkins, eds. *Cut Loose Your Stammering Tongue.* Maryknoll, N.Y.: Orbis Books, 1992.

Davis, Cyprian, and Diana L. Hayes, eds. *Taking Down Our Harps: Black Catholics in the United States.* Maryknoll, N.Y.: Orbis Books, 1998.

Davis, Gerald L. *I Got the Word in Me and I Can Sing It, You Know: A Study of the Performed African-American Sermon.* Philadelphia: University of Pennsylvania Press, 1985.

Douglas, Kelly Brown. *The Black Christ.* Maryknoll, N.Y.: Orbis Books, 1994.

———. "God Is as Christ Does: Toward a Womanist Theology." *Journal of Religious Thought* 46 (summer–fall 1989): 7–16.

———. *Sexuality and the Black Church.* Maryknoll, N.Y.: Orbis Books, 1999.

Douglass, Frederick. *Narrative of the Life of Frederick Douglass, An American Slave.* 1845; reprinted, New York: Signet Books, 1968.

Du Bois, W. E. B. *The Negro Church.* Atlanta: Atlanta University Press, 1903.

———. *The Souls of Black Folk.* 1903; reprinted, Greenwich, Conn.: Fawcett Publications, 1961.

Dyson, Michael E. *Reflecting Black: African American Cultural Criticism.* Minneapolis: University of Minnesota Press, 1993.

Earl, Riggins R., Jr. *Dark Symbols, Obscure Signs: God, Self, and Community in the Slave Mind.* Maryknoll, N.Y.: Orbis Books, 1993.

Essien-Udom, Essien Udosen. *Black Nationalism: A Search for an Identity in America.* Chicago: University of Chicago Press, 1962.

Eugene, Toinette M. "Moral Values and Black Womanism." *Journal of Religious Thought* 44 (winter–spring 1988): 23–34.

Evans, James H., Jr. *Black Theology: A Critical Assessment and Annotated Bibliography.* New York: Greenwood Press, 1987.

———. "Black Theology and Black Feminism." *Journal of Religious Thought* 38 (spring–summer 1981): 43–53.

———. "Deconstructing the Tradition: Narrative Strategies in Nascent Black Theology." *Union Seminary Quarterly Review* 44 (1990): 101–19.

———. "'I Rose and Found My Voice': Black Church Studies and Theological Education." *Theological Education* 21, no. 2 (spring 1985): 49–72.

———. *We Have Been Believers: An African American Systematic Theology.* Minneapolis: Fortress Press, 1992.

———. *We Shall All Be Changed: Social Problems and Theological Renewal.* Minneapolis: Fortress Press, 1997.

Fauset, Arthur H. *Black Gods of the Metropolis: Negro Religious Cults of the Urban North.* Philadelphia: University of Pennsylvania Press, 1944.

"The 15 Greatest Black Preachers." *Ebony* 49, no. 1 (November 1993): 156–58, 160, 162, 164, 166, 168.

"The 15 Greatest Black Women Preachers." *Ebony* 53, no. 1 (November 1997): 102–4, 106, 108, 110, 112, 114.

Frazier, E. Franklin. *The Negro Church in America.* New York: Schocken, 1963.

————, and C. Eric Lincoln. *The Negro Church in America/The Black Church since Frazier.* New York: Schocken Books, 1974.

Frazier, Thomas R. "Changing Perspectives in the Study of Afro-American Religion." *Journal of the Interdenominational Theological Center* 6 (fall 1978): 51–68.

Fulop, Timothy E., and Albert J. Raboteau, eds. *African American Religion: Interpretive Essays in History and Culture.* New York: Routledge, 1997.

Gardiner, James J., and J. Deotis Roberts, eds. *Quest for a Black Theology.* Philadelphia: United Church Press, 1971.

Gilkes, Cheryl Townsend. *If It Wasn't for the Women: Black Women's Experience and Womanist Culture in Church and Community.* Maryknoll, N.Y.: Orbis Books, 2000.

————. "Plenty Good Room: Adaptation in a Changing Black Church." *Annals of the American Academy of Political and Social Science* 558 (July 1998): 101–21.

————. "Womanist Ideals and the Sociological Imagination." *Journal of Feminist Studies in Religion* 8, no. 2 (fall 1992): 147–51.

Goatley, David Emmanuel. *Were You There? Godforsakenness in Slave Religion.* Maryknoll, N.Y.: Orbis Books, 1996.

Grant, Jacquelyn, ed. *Perspectives on Womanist Theology.* Atlanta: Interdenominational Theological Center Press, 1995.

————. "Subjectification as a Requirement for Christological Construction." In *Lift Every Voice: Constructing Christian Theologies from the Underside,* ed. Susan Brooks Thistlethwaite and Mary Potter Engel, pp. 201–13. San Francisco: Harper & Row, 1990.

————. *White Woman's Christ and Black Woman's Jesus: Feminist Christology and Womanist Response.* Atlanta: Scholars Press, 1989.

————. "Womanist Theology in North America." *Journal of the Interdenominational Theological Center* 16 (fall–spring 1988–89): 284–88.

Harris, Leonard, ed. *Philosophy Born of Struggle: Anthology of Afro-American Philosophy from 1917.* Dubuque, Iowa: Kendall/Hunt Publishing Co., 1983.

Harris, Michael W. "African American Religious History in the 1980s: A Critical Review." *Religious Studies Review* 20, no. 4 (October 1994): 263–75.

Hayes, Diana L. *Hagar's Daughters: Womanist Ways of Being in the World.* Mahwah, N.J.: Paulist Press, 1995.

————. *And Still We Rise: An Introduction to Black Liberation Theology.* Mahwah, N.J.: Paulist Press, 1996.

Herzog, Frederick. *Liberation Theology.* New York: Seabury Press, 1972.

Hodgson, Peter C. *Children of Freedom.* Philadelphia: Fortress Press, 1974.

———. *New Birth of Freedom.* Philadelphia: Fortress Press, 1976.

Hopkins, Dwight N. *Black Theology U.S.A. and South Africa.* Maryknoll, N.Y.: Orbis Books, 1989.

———. *Down, Up, and Over: Slave Religion and Black Theology.* Minneapolis: Fortress Press, 2000.

———. *Introducing Black Theology of Liberation.* Maryknoll, N.Y.: Orbis Books, 1999.

———. *Shoes That Fit Our Feet: Sources for a Constructive Black Theology.* Maryknoll, N.Y.: Orbis Books, 1993.

James, Robinson B. "Tillichian Analysis of James Cone's Black Theology." *Perspectives in Religious Studies* 1 (spring 1974): 15–28.

Johnston, Ruby F. *The Development of Negro Religion.* New York: Philosophical Library, 1954.

———. *The Religion of Negro Protestants.* New York: Philosophical Library, 1956.

Jones, Major J. *Black Awareness: A Theology of Hope.* Nashville: Abingdon Press, 1971.

———. *Christian Ethics for a Black Theology.* Nashville: Abingdon Press, 1974.

———. *The Color of God: The Concept of God in Afro-American Thought.* Macon, Ga.: Mercer University Press, 1987.

Jones, William R. "Functional Ultimacy as Authority in Religious Humanism." *Religious Humanism* 12 (winter 1978): 28–32.

———. "Is Faith in God Necessary for a Just Society? Insights from Liberation Theology." In *The Search for Faith and Justice,* 82–96, ed. Gene G. James. New York: Paragon, 1987.

———. *Is God a White Racist? A Preamble to Black Theology.* Garden City, N.Y.: Doubleday, Anchor Press, 1973.

———. "The Legitimacy and Necessity of Black Philosophy: Some Preliminary Considerations." *Philosophical Forum* 9 (winter–spring 1977–78): 149–60.

———. "Liberation Strategies in Black Theology: Mao, Martin, or Malcolm?" *Chicago Theological Seminary Register* 73 (winter 1983): 38–48.

———. "Oppression, Race, and Humanism." *The Humanist* 52, no. 6 (November–December 1992): 7–10, 32.

———. "Process Theology: Guardian of the Oppressor or Goad to the Oppressed — An Interim Assessment." *Process Studies* 18, no. 4 (winter 1989): 268–81.

———. "Religion as Legitimator and Liberator: A Worm's Eye View of Religion and Contemporary Politics." In *Spirit Matters: The Worldwide Impact of Religion on Contemporary Politics,* ed. Richard L. Rubenstein, 237–57. New York: Paragon House Publishers, 1986.

———. "Religious Humanism: Its Problems and Prospects in Black Religion and Culture." *Journal of the Interdenominational Theological Center* 7 (spring 1980): 169–86.

———. "Theism and Religious Humanism: The Chasm Narrows." *Christian Century* 92 (May 21, 1975): 520–25.

———. "Theodicy: The Controlling Category for Black Theology." *Journal of Religious Thought* 30, no. 1 (spring–summer 1973): 28–38.

———. "Theodicy and Methodology in Black Theology: A Critique of Washington, Cone, and Cleage." *Harvard Theological Review* 64, no. 4 (October 1971): 541–57.

———. "Toward a Black Theology." *Mid-Stream* 13 (fall–winter 1973–74): 2–9.

———. "Toward an Interim Assessment of Black Theology." *Christian Century* 89 (May 3, 1972): 513–17.

Kirk-Duggan, Cheryl A. *Exorcizing Evil: A Womanist Perspective on the Spirituals.* Maryknoll, N.Y.: Orbis Books, 1997.

Lee, Carleton L. "Toward a Sociology of the Black Religious Experience." *Journal of Religious Thought* 29, no. 2 (1972): 5–18.

Lincoln, C. Eric. *The Black Church since Frazier.* New York: Schocken Books, 1974.

———. *Black Muslims in America.* Boston: Beacon Press, 1961.

———. *Coming through the Fire: Surviving Race and Place in America.* Durham, N.C.: Duke University Press, 1996.

———. "Contemporary Black Religion: In Search of a Sociology," *Journal of the Interdenominational Theological Center* 5, no. 2 (spring 1978): 91–104.

———. *My Face Is Black.* Boston: Beacon Press, 1964.

———. *Race, Religion, and the Continuing American Dilemma.* New York: Hill and Wang, 1984.

———, and Lawrence H. Mamiya. *The Black Church in the African American Experience.* Durham, N.C.: Duke University Press, 1990.

Long, Charles H. "A Common Ancestor: Theology and Religious Studies." In *Religious Studies, Theological Studies, and the University-Divinity School,* ed. Joseph Kitagawa. Atlanta: Scholars Press, 1992.

———. *Significations: Signs, Symbols, and Images in the Interpretation of Religion.* Philadelphia: Fortress Press, 1986.

———. "Structural Similarities and Dissimilarities in Black and African Theologies." *Journal of Religious Thought* 33, no. 2 (fall–winter 1975): 9–24.

————. "The University, the Liberal Arts, and the Teaching and Study of Religion." In *Beyond the Classics?: Essays in Religious Studies and Liberal Education,* ed. Sheryl Burkhalter and Frank Reynolds. Atlanta: Scholars Press, 1990.

Maffly-Kipp, Laurie F. "Mapping the World, Mapping the Race: Negro Race History, 1874–1915." *Church History* 64 (December 1996): 619–26.

Matthews, Donald Henry, *Honoring the Ancestors: An African Cultural Interpretation of Black Religion and Literature.* New York: Oxford University Press, 1998.

Mays, Benjamin E., and Joseph W. Nicholson. *The Negro's Church.* New York: Institute of Social and Religious Research, 1933.

————. *The Negro's God.* Boston: Chapman & Grimes, 1938.

McGilvary, Evander B. *Toward a Perspective Realism.* The Paul Carus Lectures, 1939, ed. Albert G. Ramsperger. LaSalle, Ill.: Open Court, 1956.

Mitchell, Henry H. *Black Belief: Folk Beliefs of Blacks in America and West Africa.* New York: Harper & Row, 1975.

————, and Nicholas Cooper-Lewter. *Soul Theology: The Heart of American Black Culture.* San Francisco: Harper & Row, 1986.

Moyd, Olin P. *Redemption in Black Theology.* Valley Forge, Pa.: Judson Press, 1979.

Murphy, Larry G. "African American Christian Perspectives on Christology and Incarnation." *Ex Auditu* 7 (1991): 73–82.

————, J. Gordon Melton, and Gary L. Ward, eds. *Encyclopedia of African American Religions.* New York: Garland Publishing, 1993.

Paris, Peter J. "From Womanist Thought to Womanist Action." *Journal of Feminist Studies in Religion* 9 (spring–fall 1993): 115–25.

Payne, Wardell J., ed. *Directory of African American Religious Bodies: A Compendium by the Howard University School of Divinity.* Washington, D.C.: Howard University Press, 1991.

*The Performed Word.* Produced by Gerald L. Davis. 59 min. Memphis: Center for Southern Folklore, 1982. Videorecording.

Phelps, Jamie T., ed. *Black and Catholic: The Challenge and Gift of Black Folk: Contributions of African American Experience and Thought to Catholic Theology.* Milwaukee: Marquette University Press, 1997.

Pinn, Anthony B. *By These Hands: A Documentary History of African American Humanism.* New York: New York University Press, 2000.

————. *Varieties of African American Religious Experience.* Minneapolis: Fortress Press, 1998.

————. *Why Lord? Suffering and Evil in Black Theology.* New York: Continuum, 1995.

Poinsett, Alex. "The Quest for a Black Christ." *Ebony* 24, no. 5 (March 1969): 170–72, 174, 176, 178.

Raboteau, Albert J. *A Fire in the Bones: Reflections on African American Religious History.* Boston: Beacon Press, 1995.

———. *Slave Religion: The "Invisible Institution" in the Antebellum South.* New York: Oxford University Press, 1978.

Reist, Benjamin. *Theology in Red, White, and Black.* Philadelphia: Westminster Press, 1975.

Roberts, J. Deotis. *A Black Political Theology.* Philadelphia: Westminster Press, 1974.

———. *Black Theology in Dialogue.* Philadelphia: Westminster Press, 1987.

———. *Black Theology Today: Liberation and Contextualization.* New York: Edwin Mellon Press, 1983.

———. *Liberation and Reconciliation: A Black Theology.* Revised edition. Philadelphia: Westminster Press, 1971; reprinted, Maryknoll, N.Y.: Orbis Books, 1994.

———. *The Prophethood of Black Believers: An African American Political Theology for Ministry.* Louisville, Ky.: Westminster/John Knox Press, 1994.

———. "The Quest for Mutuality: Confronting Sexism in the Black Church: Theological Reflections on Mutuality between Black Females and Males." *AME Zion Quarterly Review* 99 (October 1988): 20–29.

———. *Roots of a Black Future: Family and Church.* Philadelphia: Westminster Press, 1980.

Rooks, Charles S. *Revolution in Zion: Reshaping African American Ministry, 1960–1974.* New York: Pilgrim Press, 1990.

———. "Toward the Promised Land: An Analysis of the Religious Experience of Black Americans." *Black Church* 2, no. 1 (1972): 1–48.

Rorty, Richard. *Philosophy and the Mirror of Nature.* Princeton, N.J.: Princeton University Press, 1979.

Ruether, Rosemary Radford. "Crisis in Sex and Race: Black Theology vs. Feminist Theology," *Christianity and Crisis* 34 (April 15, 1974): 67–73.

———. *New Woman/New Earth: Sexist Ideologies and Human Liberation.* New York: Seabury Press, 1975.

Sanders, Cheryl J. *Empowerment Ethics for a Liberated People: A Path to African-American Social Transformation.* Minneapolis: Fortress Press, 1995.

———, ed. *Living the Intersection: Womanism and Afrocentrism in Theology.* Minneapolis: Fortress Press, 1995.

———. *Saints in Exile: The Holiness-Pentecostal Experience in African American Religion and Culture.* New York: Oxford University Press, 1999.

Smith, Theophus H. *Conjuring Culture: Biblical Formations of Black America.* New York: Oxford University Press, 1994.

———. "Ethnography as Theology: Inscribing the African American Sacred Story." In *Theology without Foundations: Religious Practice and the Future of Theological Truth,* ed. Stanley Hauerwas, Nancey Murphy, and Mark Nation, 117–39. Nashville: Abingdon Press, 1994.

———. "A Phenomenological Note: Black Religion as Christian Conjuration." *Journal of the Interdenominational Theological Center* 11 (fall 1983–spring 1984): 1–18.

Stewart, Carlyle F. "The Method of Correlation in the Theology of James H. Cone." *Journal of Religious Thought* 40 (fall–winter 1983–84): 27–38.

Thiel, John E. *Nonfoundationalism.* Minneapolis: Fortress Press, 1994.

Thurman, Howard. *Deep River.* Mills College, Calif.: Eucalyptus Press, 1945.

———. *The Negro Spiritual Speaks of Life and Death.* New York: Harper, 1947.

———. *With Head and Heart: The Autobiography of Howard Thurman.* New York: Harcourt Brace Jovanovich Publishers, 1979.

Tillich, Paul. *Systematic Theology.* Vol. 1: *Reason and Revelation, Being and God.* Chicago: University of Chicago Press, 1951.

Walker, Alice. *In Search of Our Mothers' Gardens.* San Diego: Harcourt Brace Jovanovich, 1983.

Washington, James M., ed. *A Testament of Hope: The Essential Writings of Martin Luther King, Jr.* San Francisco: Harper & Row, 1986.

Washington, Joseph R., Jr. *Black Religion: The Negro and Christianity in the United States.* Boston: Beacon Press, 1964.

———. *Black Sects and Cults.* Garden City, N.Y.: Anchor Press, Doubleday, 1973.

———. *The Politics of God.* Boston: Beacon Press, 1967.

Webber, Thomas L. *Deep Like the Rivers: Education in the Slave Quarter Community, 1831–1865.* New York: W. W. Norton, 1978.

West, Cornel. *The American Evasion of Philosophy: A Genealogy of Pragmatism.* Madison: University of Wisconsin Press, 1989.

———. *Keeping Faith: Philosophy and Race in America.* New York: Routledge, 1994.

———. "Philosophy and the Afro-American Experience." *Philosophical Forum* 9 (winter–spring 1977–78): 117–48.

———. *Prophesy Deliverance! An Afro-American Revolutionary Christianity.* Philadelphia: Westminster Press, 1982.

———. *Prophetic Fragments.* Grand Rapids: Eerdmans; Trenton, N.J.: Africa World Press, 1988.

———. *Prophetic Reflections: Notes on Race and Power in America.* Vol. 2, *Beyond Eurocentrism and Multiculturalism.* Monroe, Maine: Common Courage Press, 1993.

————. *Prophetic Thought in Postmodern Times.* Vol. 1, *Beyond Eurocentrism and Multiculturalism.* Monroe, Maine: Common Courage Press, 1993.

————. *Race Matters.* Boston: Beacon Press, 1993.

Williams, Delores S. *Sisters in the Wilderness: The Challenge of Womanist God-Talk.* Maryknoll, N.Y.: Orbis Books, 1993.

Williams, Ethel L., and Clifton F. Brown. *The Howard University Bibliography of African and Afro-American Religious History.* Wilmington, Del.: Scholarly Resources, 1977.

Williams, Preston N. "An African American Perspective on the Nature and Criteria of Theological Scholarship." *Theological Education* 32 (autumn 1995): 71–78.

————. "James Cone and the Problem of a Black Ethic." *Harvard Theological Review* 65 (October 1969): 256–61.

Wilmore, Gayraud S., ed. *African American Religious Studies: An Interdisciplinary Anthology.* Durham, N.C.: Duke University Press, 1989.

————. "Black Messiah: Revising the Color Symbolism of Western Christology." *Journal of the Interdenominational Theological Center* 2 (fall 1974): 8–18.

————. "Black Religion: Strategies of Survival, Elevation, and Liberation." *Journal of the Interdenominational Theological Center* 21 (fall–spring 1993–94): 145–64.

————. *Black Religion and Black Radicalism: An Interpretation of the Religious History of Afro-American People.* 2d ed., revised and enlarged. Maryknoll, N.Y.: Orbis Books, 1983.

————. "Black Theology: Its Significance for Christian Mission Today." *International Review of Missions* 63 (April 1974): 211–31.

————. "Ethics in Black and Blight." *Christian Century* 90 (September 12, 1973): 877–78.

————. *Last Things First.* Philadelphia: Westminster Press, 1982.

Witvliet, Theo. *The Way of the Black Messiah: The Hermeneutical Challenge of Black Theology as a Theology of Liberation.* Oak Park, Ill.: Meyer-Stone, 1987.

Woodson, Carter G. *History of the Negro Church.* Washington, D.C.: Associated Publishers, 1921.

Young, Henry J. "African American Religious Thought and Revisioning Theological Methods." *Journal of Religion* 78 (April 1998): 257–65.

————. "Black Theology: Providence and Evil." *Journal of the Interdenominational Theological Center* 40, no. 2 (spring 1975): 87–96.

————. "Black Theology and the Work of William R. Jones." *Religion in Life* 44 (spring 1975): 14–28.

———. *Hope in Process: A Theology of Social Pluralism.* Minneapolis: Fortress Press, 1990.

———. *Major Black Religious Leaders since 1940.* Nashville: Abingdon Press, 1979.

———. "Process Theology and Black Liberation: Testing the Whiteheadean Metaphysical Foundations." *Process Studies* 18, no. 4 (winter 1989): 259–67.

Young, Josiah U. *Black and African Theologies.* Maryknoll, N.Y.: Orbis Books, 1986.

———. *A Pan-African Theology.* Trenton, N.J.: Africa World Press, 1992.

# Index

Human Sciences School
on blackness, 131
on content of black theology, 123–24,
142
criticism of, 153
future of, xiv, 155
on goal of black theology, 136–41,
143, 152
and human sciences approach,
116–17
on liberation, 131–32
on method of black theology, 134–36,
143, 152
on nonprivileging of blackness and
liberation, 151
on norm of black theology, 128–34,
142–43, 151
origins of, vii, 115
positive qualities of, 153–54
representative thinkers of, xii, 118–20,
141
on sources of black theology, 124–28,
142, 149–50
on tasks of black theology, 120–23,
142, 148–49
humanism, 78, 84–87
humanocentric theism
basic tenets, 93–94
consequences of, 94–97

Jones, Major J.
on relation of liberation to hope,
36
and rejection of violence in black
liberation, 60
on use of eschatology for moral
norms, 58–59
Jones, William R.
on blackness, 66, 81–82
and critique of black liberation theism,
80, 87–91
on definition and strategies of
liberation, 74, 109, 110, 112,
114
on definition of black philosophy,
66–67
on definition of humanism, 84–85

on gnosiological conversion, 109,
111
on human freedom (functional
ultimacy), 91–92
and method of internal criticism, xv,
104, 113
and resolution of the problem of
divine racism, 90–91
on tasks of black theology, 72–73
on theodicy as central category of
black theology, 79–80, 106
on theory of oppression, 107–9
on use of positive and negative
interpretations of study of religion,
8

King, Martin Luther, Jr., 2–3, 112

liberation, 131–32, 143–44, 151,
154–55
in Black Hermeneutical School, 52–55,
64
in Black Philosophical School, 74–76
as matter of ultimate concern, viii
multiple meanings of, viii, 15, 21,
26–27, 38, 149
multiple traditions of, 15–16
and related themes, 35–39, 64, 149
liberation theology, as paradigm of black
theology, vii, xii, 154–55
Lincoln, C. Eric
on black sacred cosmos, 123
on blackness, 132–33
and concerns in African American
churches, 141
on liberation as ultimate concern, 124,
143, 149, 151
on phenomenological approach to
study of religion, 132
and recommendations for academic
black theology, 141
on sociological method, 136
on tasks of theologian and sociologist,
122–23
Long, Charles H.
on black religion, 127
on blackness, 127, 129

CPSIA information can be obtained
at www.ICGtesting.com
Printed in the USA
BVHW042055260820
587411BV00013B/400

9 781556 357367